FUNDRAISING & FELLOWSHIP

Exciting Failsafe Ideas for Youth Ministry

FUNDRAISING & FELLOWSHIP

Mary Ann Zierler-Jasiak

ave maria press   Notre Dame, Indiana

Scripture texts in this work are taken from the *New American Bible with Revised New Testament and Revised Psalms* © 1991, 1986, 1970 Confraternity of Christian Doctrine, Washington, D.C. and are used by permission of the copyright owner. All Rights Reserved. No part of the *New American Bible* may be reproduced without permission in writing from the copyright owner.

© 2002 by Ave Maria Press, Inc.

All rights reserved. No part of this book may be used or reproduced in any manner whatsoever, except in the case of reprints in the context of reviews, without written permission from Ave Maria Press, Inc., P.O. Box 428, Notre Dame, IN 46556.

www.avemariapress.com

International Standard Book Number: 0-87793-959-4

Cover and text design by Brian C. Conley

Printed and bound in the United States of America.

Library of Congress Cataloging-in-Publication Data

Zierler-Jasiak, Mary Ann.
 Fundraising and fellowship : exciting failsafe ideas for youth
  ministry / Mary Ann Zierler-Jasiak.
      p. cm.
  ISBN 0-87793-959-4 (pbk.)
   1. Church group work with youth--Catholic Church. 2. Church fund
  raising. 3. Catholic Church--Finance. I. Title.
BX2347.8.Y7 Z54 2002
254'.8--dc21

2001006468
CIP

I dedicate this work to my teenage sons, Jason Charles and Jeffrey Craig Jasiak.
You have taught me so much about God's love through your humor,
your questions, and through the way you view the world.
You have been God's greatest gift to me.
I love you!

FOREWORD	9
INTRODUCTION	11
WHY WE FUNDRAISE	13
FUNDRAISING OPTIONS	14
CHOOSING YOUR FUNDRAISERS	17
DISCERNMENT RETREAT	19
FUNDRAISING EVENTS	25
SOUPER SUNDAY	27
SHARES IN THE KINGDOM	41
CANDYWORLD	57
THE STORYTELLER	69
THE BREAD BASKET	81
STRIKE UP THE BAND	95
APPENDIX	103
MORE GREAT IDEAS FOR FUNDRAISING	105

FOREWORD

The inspiration for this text came from the passion that I have for young people. As a former high school teacher, director of faith formation, and mother of two teenage sons, I have been surrounded by teens in some way, shape, or form for most of my adult life. I continue to this day to stand in awe of their humor, creativity, and ability to question and challenge. Our church has been gifted with incredible teens. All one has to do is provide opportunities for them to shine, and they will.

This book is filled with ideas to help church youth ministers, directors of religious education, or school campus ministers earn money with their teens to support and supplement their ministries. These "events" provided will not only help teens find new and interesting ways to raise money, but they will also be opportunities for prayer, reflection, and fellowship. The fundraising ideas in *Fundraising and Fellowship* really are ways for teens to shine.

Though the events were designed to help your group raise money, with slight adaptations they can also be used as service projects that do not require collecting any funds. In either case, the prayer and fellowship components of each event remain the same and will be a blessing to you, the teens, and those others in the community who will participate.

I suggest that you read the entire text, previewing all of the ideas before you choose to do any one of them first. As you read through the text, take time between each event to think about and envision how the idea will succeed at your church or school. While many of the events are more appropriate for certain specific times of the year, each can be used in a variety of times and spaces that are typical of any church or school.

INTRODUCTION

WHY WE FUNDRAISE

Most adults who work in youth ministry do not begin with the idea that fundraising will be a main part of their job description. They may imagine that all necessary funding for their programs will be provided by the teens themselves, their parents, or the larger church or school community. In many cases this may be true. Sometimes, however, the required fee for a certain event is very large. A summer mission trip or a contribution to a local charity are examples of this. Other times there is merit in having the young people earn the funding for themselves, following the familiar "allowance" principal.

Many youth ministers frown when they hear the word "fundraising." My guess for why this is so is that the task seems too time-consuming and generally one of those messy jobs that seems to offer no guarantees. One of my first suggestions is to enter into fundraising with a positive attitude. (If it helps, even think of your efforts as *fun*raising instead.) Enjoy the journey of setting and reaching a goal with teens. If you keep a positive attitude, fundraising can be an essential part of this rewarding journey.

There are many types of fundraisers to choose from. Many professional companies offer their services to provide products and directions for selling. Teens then sell a product to family, neighbors, and friends. For the most part, these types of fundraising projects are rather simple, productive for raising funds, and not very time-consuming. Most long-range plans for fundraising will include one form or another of this type of selling.

Fundraising and Fellowship suggests other ways for youth to raise money that are different from these more usual fare. What makes each of these projects or events different is that they also offer components of faith sharing, community, and prayer.

Recently, eighty of the youth at my church registered for a summer work camp in Denver. The cost for each person to attend was $450, a total of $36,000 due from our church to the organization sponsoring the work camp. It may have been tempting to have only tapped into the teens' parents and church for funding the trip. It was also probably impossible or, at least, prohibitive to do so. In this case a fundraising effort was necessary.

Teens raise money for a variety of other reasons too. Along with opportunities for mission trips and social adventures, teens also support their own ministry program as well as charitable organizations outside of the community. One youth group I knew of used a fundraiser to buy bibles for all the teens. Another had built-in fundraisers to help pay the part-time salary of their youth minister. Youth groups also are known to contribute to organizations like homeless shelters and food pantries from profits made through fundraising.

However, fundraising is not only about raising funds! There are many other communal and spiritual benefits of fundraising for parents and teens alike. Descriptions of four of these benefits follows.

1. Fundraising allows ALL young people to participate in a special event, trip, or project. Were you ever left out of a school project or class trip because you or your family could not afford the cost? It does happen to some children and teens. Just as teens are called to be advocates for all people—no matter what their economic, social, or cultural status—it is the responsibility of adults in youth ministry to be an advocate for the teens themselves, no matter what their financial status. A common fundraising effort helps to level the playing field so that all can comfortably participate.

2. Fundraising brings positive attention to your youth group. Often teenagers seem to be invisible in our local and church communities. Fundraising efforts are a very visible way to help others to see and know just how faith-filled and committed these teens are. Whenever our youth group fundraises in the local

community, people approach us out of curiosity and generosity. The teenagers have the opportunity to communicate their goals (e.g., what the raised money will be used for) as well as their very visible faith.

3. *Fundraising builds camaraderie and community among the youth.* In several churches, the teens who participate in youth ministry programs are of various ages from freshmen to seniors. Sometimes even junior high teens participate along with senior high teens. Teens from one youth group likely attend different schools. They will also have a variety of interests and friendship groups. Holding a common fundraising event helps to unify these diverse factions into one.

4. *Fundraising helps teens and adults alike to practice their faith.* The teenagers in my group are amazed when "strangers" support them—both financially and spiritually—in their endeavors. To illustrate, one time while we were on a service trip at Notre Dame, Indiana, I gathered the teens together to write thank-you letters to the adults who had supported them (see "Shares in the Kingdom," pages 41-56). One of the teens asked me "why people would want to give money to a bunch of kids they barely knew." Through a simple but profound discussion that ensued, the teens came to realize that everyone is responsible to support others in their efforts to learn about Jesus and build the kingdom of God.

These are only four reasons for fundraising. When you consider your own circumstances in working with youth, you will likely be able to add to the list. It is important to be clear about "why you fundraise." Many churches and schools prefer to keep a tight limit on the number of fundraisers in a year. Your pastor, council, board, or principal may ask you to formally present your reasons for fundraising well prior to the event itself.

Fundraising Options

Hmm, let's see. . . . A car wash or a candle sale? A raffle or a baby-sitting service? Or, maybe a pancake breakfast where we also sell raffle tickets. Decisions, decisions.

It's really no secret that a major key to success with teens is tapping into their unique talents while all the while acknowledging their different skills. For example, I know some teens who can sell a case of candy bars in one hour. On the other hand, I also know that there is a full case of those same candy bars (from last year's fundraiser) sitting in the closet of another teen.

Regarding fundraising options, the real question is "What type of fundraising is best suited to the talents, interests, and needs of the group?" Listed below are some various types of fundraising. Read through each option, keeping the particulars of your own group in mind.

Selling

Fundraising companies provide many options for selling. A group can sell things like cookie dough, flavored coffee, frozen pizza, cheese, candles, ice cream cake certificates, wrapping paper, fruit, magazines, candy bars, and much more. All of these endeavors have some degree of profitability as the group is able to keep a designated amount. They also require little work by the organizer and are generally easy to bring to a conclusion.

Comments: Teens who seem to do the best at this type of fundraising are those with large, extended families or those whose parents work in office situations where soliciting is acceptable. This is also a negative for this type of fundraising as it is often the parents who do most of the selling on behalf of their children. Too much selling and buying can also be a burden on your church and school community as many other organizations seem to use this method. Burnout—including pocketbook burnout—may occur.

Local Business Opportunities

Many local businesses offer special opportunities for teens to earn money. For example, an Italian restaurant in our area allows teens to serve breadsticks and bus tables for tips. Also, a department store nearby recruits teens to bag merchandise during the Christmas season while asking the customers to make donations to the teen's organization.

Comments: A benefit of this form of fundraising is that the teens are out in the community and the public is able to interact with them about the reason they are trying to earn money. Finding opportunities through your local businesses may take time, but once you do you will likely be able to tap into them more than once.

Matching Funds and Grants

Many businesses have matching funds programs. This means that if you raise money by selling candy bars, the business will match whatever profit your group has earned. Wal-Mart has traditionally sponsored such a program. You can encourage the parents of your teens to check with their employers to see if they would be willing to sponsor such a matching funds program.

Grants, on the other hand, are monies given to assist charitable organizations for any efforts that will benefit the community at large. Many businesses allocate a certain amount of their budget to donate to groups like yours. A letter proposing your request for funding along with what the funding will be used for may bring a positive response.

Comments: Except for the fact that the teens may be asked to describe their reason for needing funds in a letter or presentation, this type of fundraiser has little or no youth involvement. However, it is a great avenue to communicate the work your teens are involved in to the community and business leaders. It is helpful to secure an adult with experience in writing proposals for grants and matching funds.

Donations by Charitable Agencies

Related to local business opportunities and grant writing, you or your group can write or make a personal presentation to a charitable agency for donations to support an area of your ministry. Agencies like the Knights of Columbus, Lions Club, and local veterans' clubs apply. If possible, have the teens compose the letters or make the presentations to these groups themselves.

Comments: This is a simple project that may only require a letter of request and a thank-you note. On the other hand, these agencies receive many requests for donations, so your inquiry may not be responded to immediately, if at all. However, it is certainly worth making the effort as it offers another way to publicize your program and the activities your teens are involved in.

Charging for a Service

You are probably already very familiar with opportunities that fit in this category—everything from car washes, to baby-sitting services, to running errands, to doing yard work. A good deal of planning and publicity are required for each of these service events. But upon doing so you can expect a fair to good monetary return on your efforts.

Comments: I have found that young people truly enjoy events of this kind. They seem to value the time together working for a common cause. I usually include at least one of these types of events per year in our fundraising efforts.

The rest of this book contains ideas for **special projects** that do not fit comfortably in any of the above fundraising categories. Each of these special projects includes ways for the teens to really be involved in the work itself, many opportunities to interact with parishioners and community members of all ages, and of course built-in chances for prayer, faith-sharing, and fellowship.

Please preview each of the special projects listed in the rest of the book as you make your fundraising decisions for the program year ahead. The "Discernment Retreat" on pages 19-24 can help you and your teens prayerfully make the best decisions for your group.

Choosing Your Fundraisers

Discernment Retreat

As with other parts of youth ministry, it is best to involve the teens in the process for choosing fundraisers. Choosing their own fundraisers helps teens take ownership of their success. While this text provides you and your teens with proven ideas for fundraising, by allowing the teens to discern which they will use they will quickly make them their own.

A discernment retreat provides a prayerful means to discern and choose which fundraisers your group would like to hold. The teens will be able to prayerfully reflect on issues that touch their hearts, as well as their own talents and ways they might combine these with any fundraising efforts.

The short discernment retreat suggested here is for teens in your program. You may also include parents and adult volunteers.

Discernment Retreat Agenda and Instructions for Leaders

The following is a point-by-point retreat agenda. You can use all or some of these suggestions and arrange them to best suit the discernment efforts of your group.

1. Welcome
Make nametags available. Greet the teens and adults as they arrive.

2. Icebreaker: Create a Story
Holding a hat in your hands, begin a story with "Once upon a time there was a young man who overslept and. . . ." Then hand the hat to the next person and ask him or her to add to the story. Continue so that the hat is handed to everyone in the group and all have a chance to add to the story. After the last person, retrieve the hat and conclude the story with "And the young man went back to bed" or some other ending of your own choosing.

3. Prayer
Distribute copies of the prayer sheet "Jesus' Spirit Is With Us" (pages 22-23). Assign parts to the participants and pray it together.

4. Witness Talk
Ask someone from your local or church community with experience in fundraising for charitable or nonprofit organizations to share some of his or her experience with the group. Ask the person to speak about the hard work and commitment it takes to be successful as well as the satisfaction they receive

from participating in worthwhile fundraising projects. True stories, anecdotes, and other words of encouragement are also appropriate to share.

5. Teen Sharing

Invite teens who have participated in previous fundraising ventures to share their insights as well as some positive stories that illustrate the experience for them.

6. Stretch and Hospitality Break

Provide light snacks and drinks and a chance for the participants to move around.

7. Brainstorming Session

With the group, brainstorm several ideas for fundraising. Include the ideas described in this book by providing the following background information on each in your discussion:

Souper Sunday

Teens and adult volunteers prepare a variety of soups to sell to parishioners after Sunday Mass. Other menu items may include bread, salads, beverages, and desserts. These "meals" are offer on a "sit in" or "take out" basis.

On a different scale, the meal may be advertised in the outlying community with people in and outside of the church being invited.

Shares in the Kingdom

Teens sell "shares" (like stock shares) in themselves. In order to sell these shares, the teens invite adults (parishioners) to a meeting to hear about the proposed use for the funds. The teens keep these "shareholders" abreast of how their funds are being used through the course of the year or one specific event.

At the end of the year or event, the teens meet again with the shareholders to give a final report, which may include playing a video or performing a short skit.

Candyworld

Teens and adult volunteers make specialty candy and cookies to sell, usually during the holiday season. At the same time, the teens create a life-sized "Candyworld" game board on the floor of an auditorium or gymnasium.

Paid admission to play the game is charged to families with younger children. The cookies and candy are eaten and sold as part of playing the game.

The Storyteller

Working in small groups, the teens practice reciting and performing popular children's stories. Parents, grandparents, and young children are invited to the final performance and asked to make a donation.

The Bread Basket

In a common kitchen (for example, in the church hall), teens gather to make fresh breads of all kinds. When ready, the teens package and sell the breads at the church or at a neighborhood bazaar.

The teens attach an appropriate scripture quotation to each package.

Strike Up the Band

Teens organize a concert where admission is charged. Various types of bands can be used for the concert, including school bands or orchestras or local rock bands or ensembles made up of teens.

For the concert, ice cream, pies, T-shirts, or other items can be sold for a profit.

Write each of the brainstormed ideas on a board or piece of poster paper where all can see. Keep the ideas free-flowing, but eventually narrow them to the top three choices. Record the top three ideas on a separate sheet of paper which you will keep.

8. Small Group Discernment

In preselected small groups, have the participants discuss the three top ideas that were brainstormed, listing positive and negative reactions on a large sheet of poster paper. Finally, ask them to come to a consensus of which idea they are most enthused about and most willing to participate in as a fundraiser.

9. Small Group Reports

Call on a representative from each small group to share their decision with all the participants, including the reasons for deciding as they did. After all the groups have reported, thank them for their efforts and tell them that you will report back to them which fundraiser(s) you will do. Explain that due to feasibility issues, the final choice will be yours (and the pastor, principal, or whomever else you are responsible to). Of course, if consensus is such and you are able, you may be able to determine which project(s) you will undertake at this time. Use the "Planning Calendar" (page 24) to pencil in your plans.

10. Video Presentation (optional)

Choose and play a video like *Mother Teresa* by Red Rose Gallerie (1986). The video shows Mother Teresa serving the poor on the streets of Calcutta and serving as advocate for the poor around the world. Lead a discussion on the participants' reaction to the video when it is completed.

11. Final Prayer

Join hands and sing a closing song or simply recite the Lord's Prayer together.

Jesus' Spirit Is With Us

Leader: Remembering that we are in God's presence, let us pause to pray before we begin our discernment.

Reader 1: When Jesus began his ministry in Galilee, he quoted from the scriptures to express what his earthly mission would be. The gospel of Luke records this story.

Proclaimer: A reading from the gospel of Luke.

He stood up to read and was handed a scroll of the prophet Isaiah. He unrolled the scroll and found the passage where it was written: "The Spirit of the Lord is upon me, because he has anointed me to bring glad tidings to the poor. He has sent me to proclaim liberty to captives and recovery of sight to the blind, to let the oppressed go free, and to proclaim a year acceptable to the Lord." Rolling up the scroll, he handed it back to the attendant and sat down, and the eyes of all in the synagogue looked intently at him. He said to them, "Today this scripture passage is fulfilled in your hearing."

The gospel of the Lord.

All: Praise to you Lord Jesus Christ.

Reader 2: Let us think about how Jesus fulfilled his promise through his life, death, and resurrection. Let us pray: Lord, you brought glad tidings to the poor and the love of the Father to all. Help us to do the same.

All: We promise to spread your good tidings to all.

Reader 3: Lord, in your healings of the sick, you brought hope to those who thought they were unloved or even cursed by God. You brought freedom to the captives. Help us to do the same.

All: We promise to spread your good tidings to all.

Reader 4: Lord, by your death and resurrection you have now set all generations free. You have empowered us to carry on your mission.

All: We promise to spread your good tidings to all.

Jesus' Spirit Is With Us

Reader 5: Because we believe that the Spirit of Jesus is with us, let us take turns completing the following statement: **Because the Spirit of Jesus is with us, I believe that we can. . . .**

(Allow each person the chance to speak. If the group is large, have each person simply share with a person sitting close by.)

Reader 6: Lord, we thank you for being with us today. We ask your blessings on our discernment and planning retreat. Help us to remember that you are at the center of everything we do. Please guide our decisions and give us the courage to do your will. We ask this in your name.

All: Amen.

Jesus' Spirit Is With Us

It's our turn to bring glad tidings to the world!

Planning Calendar

Pencil in your plan.

January
   What: _____
   When: _____

February
   What: _____
   When: _____

March
   What: _____
   When: _____

April
   What: _____
   When: _____

May
   What: _____
   When: _____

June
   What: _____
   When: _____

July
   What: _____
   When: _____

August
   What: _____
   When: _____

September
   What: _____
   When: _____

October
   What: _____
   When: _____

November
   What: _____
   When: _____

December
   What: _____
   When: _____

Jesus' Spirit Is With Us!

Fundraising Events

Souper Sunday

(Teenagers gather to prepare soups, bread "bowl" salads, and desserts
to serve the church community and other invited guests.)

Background

Okay, I know you are wondering "Why soup?"

Think about it. Close your eyes and ponder the word "soup" for a moment. Does it bring any special memories to mind? Is there a family member who made your favorite recipe and allowed you to chop the ingredients for it? Perhaps your mom or dad brought you a bowl of soup when you were sick or prepared some for an ailing neighbor or friend.

For me, my memories are very vivid. Before there were automatic food processors my sisters, brother, and I were the original "vegetable choppers." My mom and grandmother (who lived with us) made wonderful chicken, split pea, and celery soups.

Today, it doesn't surprise me that one of the best-selling series of books for reflection and renewal is called *Chicken Soup for the Soul*. In our hectic world, soup brings about thoughts of friendship, well-being, and taking time out. To get the full flavor of the ingredients, soup has to simmer. Unlike many of the fast foods we are now accustomed to, eating a wonderful bowl of soup takes patience. I have yet to see a person driving and eating a hot bowl of soup at the same time.

In answering the question "Why soup?" I also refer you to the beloved tale *Stone Soup*. It depicts love, community, and trust and portrays the power of people working together for the common good. *Stone Soup* reminds me of Jesus' feeding of the thousands and, ultimately, Eucharist.

In summary, to provide a Souper Sunday experience as a fundraiser, you are not only raising money for your youth ministry program, but also building community with your young people and their families in a wholesome and fun way. And, of course, your patrons will benefit from this fundraiser by being served a simple but tasty meal made with love.

What Is a Souper Sunday?

Imagine this scene:

Early on a Saturday morning, your youth and adult participants meet in the church or school cafeteria. The eyes of the teenagers are not completely open yet, but the teens themselves are in good spirits. They have come bearing not only a willingness to participate, but they have also brought vegetables and other ingredients for the soup with them. After a prayer of thanksgiving for the food items and fellowship, the work begins.

Since you have preselected two or three soups and have gathered all the ingredients together, you are now able to put everyone to work washing, peeling, chopping, and boiling. Of course, if you are serving side dishes such as the suggested bread bowl salads and desserts, those items will also need to be prepared. It is amazing how it works, but the young people do find something they like to do and they do it well. I've been working on Souper Sundays for years, and the teenagers never cease to amaze me.

Now, flash ahead to Sunday morning. Because the teens have worshiped with their families the night before, they arrive early to decorate, do last minute food preparations, and greet their customers. Just before you open your doors for the event, you join hands to ask God for his blessings on the food and those who will share it. The arriving patrons are impressed with the youth for their awesome hospitality as well as their terrific service. There is no doubt that the soup, made through the hard work of many hands, is the best ever. You can tell because your customers would like to take some home for a friend or for themselves.

Finally, the rush is over and your patrons are asking the teens when they will be hosting another Souper Supper and if they would please make their favorite soups again. Feeling very tired yet very affirmed, the teens respond positively. As you and the teens are washing the dishes and cleaning up, you are able to talk with the young people about their experiences. It seems like each one has their own story of an individual who was very complimentary or who told them a great joke.

And you? You are exhausted and you smell a great deal like the soup that has been prepared and served, but you are amazed at how God works in your life and in the lives of the teenagers. Did you earn enough money for the event to reach your goal? Sure. But you did so much more besides.

Getting Started

The more you are able to involve the teens in the planning and preparation of the event, the more ownership they will feel for the event itself.

If you are able to include your core group or a committee made up of youth for planning purposes, meet with them well prior to any dates you are considering for the event.

The "Souper Sunday Planning Meeting Agenda" (pages 29-30) provides a suggested list of items to cover as well as a short prayer service to accompany the meeting.

The "Souper Sunday Quickstart" (pages 31-32) provides basic and sequential information for putting on the event as well as a list of tasks that will help you get started, with or in lieu of a planning meeting.

Souper Sunday Planning Meeting Agenda

The following is a point-by-point meeting agenda. You can use all or some of these suggestions and arrange them to best suit your needs. You can also record decisions made at the meeting in the spaces provided.

1. Welcome

Greet the participants. Distribute copies of the word puzzle "Great Soups and Great Disciples" (page 33) for the participants to play while waiting for everyone to arrive.

2. Prayer

Use the prayer service, "Your Light Must Shine" (page 34).

3. Dates and Times

Brainstorm some possible weekends that will work well for a Souper Sunday event. Take into account school and church schedules in your planning. Record four possible weekends below.

1.   3.
2.   4.

4. Other menu items to decide "yea" or "nay" on

Circle the group's consensus.

Beverages	Yes	No
Desserts	Yes	No
Bread	Yes	No
Bread Bowls	Yes	No
Other	Yes	No

5. Assign responsibility for arranging for donations of the following ingredients and supplies

Write the name(s) of the person(s) next to each item.

Dairy

Bakery

Grocery

Meat

Paper Products

6. **Determine where these parts of the event will take place**
    Write the group's consensus below.

    The preparation of the soup

    The sale of the soup

7. **Determine the prices for the soup and other items**
    Will you sell by quantity or offer discount prices for children?

8. **How will the event be advertised? Who are people in the church and local community who can help with promotion?**
    Write some ideas discussed and the name of the person assigned the responsibility for coordinating decorations.

    Ideas:

    Person Responsible:

9. **How will the place be decorated?**
    Write some ideas discussed and the name of the person assigned the responsibility for coordinating advertising.

    Ideas:

    Person Responsible:

10. **Other issues the group counts as important**
    Write the ideas below.

11. **Closing Prayer**
    Say:
    Father, we thank you for being with us at this meeting. We ask your blessings on each of us in the days ahead and your guidance so that we might be a light on behalf of everyone we come in contact with. We ask this in the name of your Son, Jesus, our Lord.

    All: Amen.

Souper Sunday Quickstart

The following list offers sequential planning steps and directions for the "Souper Supper" event. The list also provides references to other resource material that you may use to plan for and hold the event. Try to involve the teens in as many of these steps as you can.

1. Check local restaurant/health regulations to find out how wide of scope the event can take on. If your church is without a restaurant license, the event may have to be limited to your local church community.

2. Using the church and school calendars as a guide, select a date and time for the event that will not conflict in a great way with other events. Schedule the kitchen and serving space you will use. Be sure to allot enough time for food preparation, decorating, serving, and cleanup. Also, check to see if the kitchen space includes cooking utensils such as peelers, knives, pots, and the like.

3. Select two or three different soups to prepare for your guests. Decide how much of each recipe to prepare. (Sample recipes are included on pages 35-37.) If there are any "master" soup makers in your church or school communities, be sure to invite them to be part of the "cooking team."

4. Decide what food items you would like to serve with the soup, for example, a bread bowl salad (directions included on page 37), beverages, and a dessert. A separate group of teens can make the dessert while others are making the soup. (A recipe for carrot cake is also included on page 37.)

5. Determine how much you will charge for the soup and other items. For example, you may charge per meal, by age, by quantities, or by separate food items.

6. Solicit donations from local businesses of ingredients and other supplies for the event. Make a list of bakery, dairy, grocery, and paper products you will need. Form a committee to solicit donations.

7. Develop an advertising plan for both within and outside the church community. A sample bulletin announcement is included on page 38.

8. Decide on the type of dishes and utensils that will be used. Real dishes and silverware are recommended if possible as they are better for the environment and lend more "class" to the event.

9. Plan on decorating the serving area in colors that are appropriate for the season of the year. Recommendation: Use brightly colored place mats as well as twisted crepe paper down the center of each table. Also, you can make copies of the "Great Soups and Great Disciples Word Search" (page 33) to use as place mats. This will give the customers something to do while they wait for their meal to be served.

10. Put a tip jar with a dollar bill in it on each table. You will be surprised how the teens' great service will encourage tipping.

11. For the meal preparation itself, plan to organize the teens into small work groups to do things like peel, chop, and clean ingredients for the soup. Other groups can prepare bread bowls or make desserts.

12. Let the teens sign up for jobs that they would like to do during the actual event such as greeters, hosts, servers, take-out managers, and cashiers. Instruct the teens on the importance of friendliness and engaging the customers in conversation.

13. On the day of the event itself, pray with the teens before the customers arrive. The resource "Give Them Some Food Yourselves" (page 39) is one option for prayer.

14. Plan on a hard day of work but also having lots of fun!

15. All the teens should help with cleanup. After the space is completely cleaned, distribute the "Souper Sunday Evaluation" (page 40) to each teen. Have them fill it out at home and return it at a later time.

GREAT SOUPS AND GREAT DISCIPLES WORD SEARCH

Find the following words in the puzzle below.

onions	celery	carrots	water	cheese
chicken	ham	beef	clams	mushrooms
milk	corn	peas	stock	salt
pepper	butter	potatoes	flour	squash
cream	parsley	tomatoes	pasta	love
faith	hope	charity	compassion	forgiveness
humility	service	wisdom	knowledge	reverence
courage	right-judgement	wonder	understanding	honesty
joy	patience	encouragement	trust	humor
concern	prayerfulness	loyalty		

```
M I L K N O W L E D G E C O G H Z L H U M O R N D L O U P A S T A
A U S P W R K O J M J C O N C E R N E U X N B A Z W R I Y A O O V
S I S T H G W T A I C V M X H F R E H O H I L O I P W I S D O M E
M I Q H E G B O H A M X P O E L O T F I J O Y W K S D N O T Y A C
T H U T R U S T F G R Z A X E Y U I V S E N R W C Y H O N E S T Y
D C A R R O I B N M H E S W S T R Y U I O S C C R D U P K L M O S
C I S O U A O V P I J Y S W E A L P E P P E R C H U M P R O T E F
E X H U F A O M K L I D I R T E J G B W E E T Y U W I D O P T S O
T Y X Q F R I D S O S T O C K W A S T U A D G E E F L O U R A U R
E R T G Y H I O P T R E N O P R E I L M A W Q U I I L O P H J G G
C H I C K N P O E Y I N B R M I L P C A R R A T B U T T E R W X I
L O M E H U M O P A T I E N C E K N W L E D G R U S Y T S H O A V
A M R C H I C K E N P S A T A L O V E R I C R E A C X C E H J R E
M N V A U N D R S Y A N I O P H J H Q W I E T N W A T E R J U L N
S I R R W Q A V E L A B N D A D D I S O N N C L R A K L V J K I E
C O R R N P R A Y E R F U L N E S S P P B G H R B B O E I T W R S
N O G O B C T O T A T O E C L K J I O J F K I S E Y T R C A B L S
L Y A T R R I G H T J U D G E M E N T K H J U Y E C C Y E A S D H
O L O S E L E N N Y P I C K E H L X A T Y U I O F S A M S A S O W
Y U H L V T E R D H N M U N D E R S T A N D I N G S P O G E P O U
A L T U E J S M X K Y H M E W R O W O T W R N R G J C H R E E S T
L B P A R S L E Y C O N R I A N B C E X H G D T R E R E C D A M P
T K L W E V A T I O N P E G H H E R S A L T O G H R D A F T S T R
Y O R I N U I L A B C X Y G U H P Y X F R U G L A N O I P E S A D
I H A S C O U R A G E E N C O U R A G E M E N T O U R G E A E N C
C L A H E M S F L O U Y C H A R I T Y O M A D W O E S W H A T C R
```

33

Your Light Must Shine

Prayer Service

Leader: Lord, we have gathered in your name to plan a special meal for our community. Be with us as you promised. Help us to remember that our goal is to serve you and your people as we listen to your word.

Proclaimer: A reading from the gospel of Matthew.

"You are the light of the world. A city set on a mountain cannot be hidden. Nor do they light a lamp and then put it under a bushel basket; it is set on a lampstand, where it gives light to all in the house. Just so, your light must shine before others, that they may see your good deeds and glorify your heavenly Father."

The gospel of the Lord.

All: **Praise to you, Lord Jesus Christ.**

Leader: Let us reflect quietly for a moment on a specific gift that God has given us to help us be light to the world.

(Allow the chance for the participants to share their gifts, either with the group at large or with a partner. After the sharing time the leader continues.)

Lord, thank you for these gifts. Help us to use them in ways that serve ourselves, others, and you. We ask this in your name.

All: **Amen.**

Soup Recipes

Cheddar Ham Chowder
This recipe will make one large kettle of soup (about 25 bowls).

8 c. water
8 c. cubed, peeled potatoes
2 c. sliced carrots
1 c. chopped onion
2 c. chopped celery
4 tsp. salt
1 tsp. pepper

1 c. margarine/butter (2 sticks)
1 c. flour
8 c. milk (1/2 gallon)
8 c. shredded cheddar cheese
4 8-oz. cans of corn, drained
6 c. cubed, fully cooked ham

In a large soup pot bring the ingredients in the left hand column to a boil. Reduce heat and simmer for 15 minutes or until tender.

In a pan about the size of a Dutch oven, melt margarine or butter. Blend in flour. Add the milk all at once; cook and stir until thick. Add cheese. Stir into the undrained cooked vegetables. Add corn and ham. Heat slowly. Reheat slowly, adding hot water if too thick.

Cream of Asparagus Soup
*A great untraditional soup for your menu.
This recipe will make about 20 bowls.*

4 lbs. (12 c.) asparagus
8-12 chicken bouillon cubes
1 c. butter or margarine
1 c. flour

8 c. milk
salt
pepper

Chop asparagus in 1/2 inch pieces. Add water to almost cover the asparagus in the pot. Add chicken bouillon cubes. Cover and cook until tender.

In another saucepan, melt butter/margarine. Stir in the flour slowly. Slowly add the milk. Cook until smooth, then add to asparagus in the pot. Salt and pepper to taste.

Soup Recipes

Butternut Squash Soup
This recipe will make about 24 bowls.

9 lbs. unpeeled butternut squash, halved and seeded
6 lg. unpeeled onions
3 sm. garlic bulbs
3/4 c. olive or vegetable oil
2 tsp. dried thyme
9 to 11 1/2 c. chicken broth
1 1/2 c. whipping cream
1/2 c. minced fresh parsley
1 1/2 tsp. salt
3/4 tsp. pepper

Cut squash into 24 large pieces. Place cut sides up in several baking pans. Cut 1/4 in. off tips of onion and garlic bulbs (off the end that comes to a closed point). Place cut sides up in a baking pan. Brush squash, onion, and garlic with oil; sprinkle with thyme. Cover pans tightly and bake at 350 degrees for 1 1/2 to 2 hours or until vegetables are very tender. Uncover and let stand until lukewarm. Remove peel from squash and onions. Remove soft garlic from skins.

Combine vegetables, broth, and cream. Purée in small batches in a blender or food processor until smooth. Transfer to large soup pot. Add parsley, salt, and pepper. Heat through (do not boil).

Zucchini Soup
This recipe will make about one Dutch oven of soup.

1 1/2 lb. ground beef, browned with onion
2 c. celery, cut up
5 to 6 c. cubed zucchini
1 large onion
7 c. canned or fresh tomatoes
2 to 4 c. of water
2 tsp. salt
1 tsp. Italian seasoning
1 tsp. oregano
1 tsp. sugar
1 tsp. basil
1/2 tsp. garlic salt

Mix all and bring to a boil. Simmer for 1 hour.

Soup Recipes

Directions for Bread Bowl Salads

1. Thaw one pound loaves of regular bread dough (in a pan covered with plastic wrap) overnight. Cut each loaf into 4 or 5 equal pieces. Spray aluminum tart pans lightly with cooking spray. Gently pull dough to fit and shape over pans. (These will be as different as snowflakes.) Let rise slightly.

2. Spray a baking sheet. Fit as many tart pans (reusable) on the sheet as possible.

3. Bake at 350 degrees for about 20 minutes or until the bread is lightly brown. (Cool and store in plastic bags if these are made a day ahead of time.)

4. Fill with lettuce and other salad ingredients.

Vicki's Awesome Carrot Cake Recipe
Young people are great at preparing this!

1. Mix together:
   - 2 c. flour
   - 2 c. sugar
   - 2 tsp. baking soda
   - 1 tsp. salt
   - 1 tsp. cinnamon

2. Now add and mix together:
   - 1 1/2 c. vegetable oil

3. Add:
   - 4 eggs (one at a time)

4. Now stir in:
   - 3 c. grated carrots

5. Spray either a 9" x 13" pan (for a high cake) or a jelly roll pan (for a bar type cake) with vegetable oil.

6. Bake at 350 degrees for 30 minutes to one hour depending on the depth of your pan or when a toothpick comes out clean.

Cream Cheese Frosting
Mix together:
- 1/2 c. melted butter
- 1 8-oz. pkg. cream cheese
- 1 tsp. vanilla

Then add and mix in
- 1 lb. powdered sugar

Cool and frost the cake.

37

Sample Bulletin Announcement

Because the Holy Name Youth have planned a service trip to Denver, Colorado . . .

Please join us for our second annual

SOUPER SATURDAY/SUNDAY

What: An awesome lunch or dinner of soup, bread bowl salads, beverages, and desserts served by your favorite church teenagers. The soups featured will be hearty beef vegetable, chili, and chicken vegetable.

When: Saturday, February 10 (following the 4:15 p.m. liturgy)
Sunday, February 11 from 11 a.m. to 1 p.m.

Where: The Holy Name Cafeteria

How much: $6.00 for adults
$3.00 for children under 12
Meals include soup, bread, and beverage.
Salads and desserts are extra.

Why: Our youth group is earning money in order to participate in the Catholic Heart Workcamp in Denver in July. The money will defray the registration and travel costs.

GIVE THEM SOME FOOD YOURSELVES

Prayer Service
Hold this prayer service with the teens approximately one-half hour before the start of the event.

Leader: Lord, we have come together in your name to serve your people. Help us to remember that we are in your presence this very moment and every moment of our lives. Knowing this, let us listen to your word with an open mind and open heart. We ask this in your name.

All: **Amen.**

Proclaimer: A reading from the gospel of Luke.

When the apostles returned, they explained to him what they had done. He took them and withdrew in private to a town called Bethsaida. The crowds, meanwhile, learned of this and followed him. He received them and spoke to them about the kingdom of God, and he healed those who needed to be cured. As the day was drawing to a close, the Twelve approached him and said, "Dismiss the crowd so that they can go to the surrounding villages and farms and find lodging and provisions; for we are in a deserted place here." He said to them, "Give them some food yourselves." They replied, "Five loaves and two fish are all we have, unless we ourselves go and buy food for all these people." Now the men there numbered about five thousand. Then he said to his disciples, "Have them sit down in groups of [about] fifty." They did so and made them all sit down. Then taking the five loaves and the two fish, and looking up to heaven, he said the blessing over them, broke them, and gave them to the disciples to set before the crowd. They all ate and were satisfied. And when the leftover fragments were picked up, they filled twelve wicker baskets.

The gospel of the Lord.

All: **Praise to you, Lord Jesus Christ.**

Leader: Lord, we ask your blessings on the soup that we have prepared in your name. May those who share in this feast have their fill of both our soup and our love. By this act of service may we model the love you have for us to all who come to us. We ask this in your name.

All: **Amen.**

Before the guests arrive, have everyone (teens and adult volunteers) join hands and pray the Our Father.

Souper Sunday Evaluation

Name _____

1. Name four things that you liked about the Souper Sunday event.

2. How can this event be improved?

3. Share one positive experience you had interacting with a customer on Souper Sunday.

4. What evidence did you find of God's blessing on this event?

Shares in the Kingdom

(Teens sell shares of stock in themselves for a specific event and patrons become investors in the next generation of adult disciples.)

Background

When someone asked basketball star Michael Jordan how he was able to achieve great success, he responded, "I visualized where I wanted to be, the kind of player I wanted to become. I knew exactly where I wanted to go and focused on getting there." Jordan knew that having success in reaching his goals would take a deliberate and focused effort. I believe that being a disciple of Christ and training future disciples is like that.

When I interview teens at the end of their preparation for the sacrament of confirmation, I ask them how they plan to carry out their faith as they go off to college, trade school, or into the adult work force. I ask them about how they will continue to worship at Sunday Mass, how they will find time to pray, and what they will do to serve others. The teens soon come to realize that what I am getting at is that being a disciple of Christ takes thought, planning, time, and effort. They have to decide what kind of adult Catholics they will be and how they will accomplish their goals. "Shares in the Kingdom" is an event where teens can witness firsthand the responsibility and care adults in the church community have for their own faith life.

What Is "Shares in the Kingdom"?

"Shares in the Kingdom" is a very deliberate way teenagers can say to their church community, family, and friends that they want to explore what it is like to walk in the footsteps of Jesus and the first disciples. This fundraiser describes to the community what the funds will be used for (e.g., program or special event) and asks parishioners to buy shares (make a dollar pledge) in a particular teen. It also puts these adult "shareholders" into direct contact with the teens they are sponsoring.

This is a great fundraiser to encourage collaboration among all generations in the church. It helps teens witness what is meant by an adult commitment to faith—a choice they must make for themselves.

Getting Started

There is no need for a planning meeting with teens for this event. The "Shares in the Kingdom Quickstart" (page 42) provides chronological directions for this fundraiser. A key to this fundraiser is to make the teens and their activities visible among the faith community (e.g., through Mass attendance, sponsoring sales outside of Mass, service projects, presentations at church meetings, etc.) and effective advertisement of the fundraiser itself.

Shares in the Kingdom Quickstart

The following list offers sequential planning steps and directions for the "Shares in the Kingdom" event. The list also provides references to other resource material that you may use to plan for and hold the event. Try to involve the teens in as many of these steps as you can.

1. Set dates for the start and end of this fundraiser, for example October to April. If you decide to do this as an annual event, keep the same time every year. Many of the contributors may be on fixed incomes and can put this fundraiser into their budget for charitable expenditures. You may also consider doing a shorter version of this fundraiser during Lent as it can be part of a family's almsgiving for the season.

2. Advertise the event. If possible, include a bulletin insert (see sample on page 44) on a Sunday well before the start of the fundraiser. Put updates on the teens' activities in the bulletin often throughout the duration.

3. The teens are to recruit adults to be shareholders to monetarily sponsor their program activities or special project. Allow the teens the opportunity to begin recruiting shareholders well before the introductory shareholder's meeting (see Sample Shareholder's Meeting Notes on page 43). To help in this process, design share certificates and record-keeping sheets (see pages 45-47). Other adults will come forward to volunteer from bulletin announcements and the like. Share certificates are given to the adult shareholders and the amount of money pledged is printed on the record-keeping sheets.

4. Invite the adults who have made pledges to come to the introductory shareholder's meeting. Remind the teens that they must attend this meeting. Their adult shareholders will be anxious to meet them face to face and hear about how their money will be used. The teens will also be needed to provide hospitality at the meeting.

5. During the duration of the fundraiser, have the teens stay in contact with the shareholders. This can typically happen through letter-writing and e-mail correspondence, though the teens may occasionally invite the shareholders to one or more youth events.

6. Conclude the fundraiser with a second shareholder's meeting. Incorporate some of the same elements from the introductory meeting. In addition, for the concluding meeting choose several teens to offer testimonials about their participation in the youth ministry program or special event. If possible, have the teens prepare skits or videos that depict a review of their activities. When the meeting has concluded, have the teens fill out a "Shares in the Kingdom Evaluation" (page 56).

Sample Shareholder's Meeting Notes

The following notes are a sample of a particular Shareholder's Meeting. Adapt the notes to fit your group. Many of these suggestions can be applied to either an introductory meeting for shareholders or a concluding celebration of the programming year/event in appreciation of the shareholders.

Purpose: To introduce the concept of adults pledging and purchasing shares for youth ministry or to thank shareholders who have already helped to sponsor youth ministry programming or a special project.

Theme: For example, "Teen Pilgrims."

Background: The meeting/celebration is a gathering of adults who plan to or are already participating as "shareholders" in church youth ministry. To fit the theme, the teens provide homemade desserts from around the world to celebrate their own pilgrimage of faith (see pages 48-50 for sample recipes). The teens will also offer testimonials of their experiences in youth ministry.

Environment: The meeting space should be decorated as festively as possible. Colored place mats and matching crepe paper work well. Short stories of Christian heroes can be used as part of the place setting. (See pages 51-53) for samples of Christian heroes bios. The teens can also be assigned to research and create their own short reports to use for place mats.) Randomly placed photos of the teens involved in youth ministry are also a nice touch. On the refreshment table, place a bible, candle, and globe to symbolize the universality of the church along with placards describing the country of origin for each dessert.

Preparation: For an introductory shareholder's meeting, have the teens invite their shareholders when they are taking pledges. For a concluding meeting, have the teens send out invitations at least one month ahead of time. Assign the teens to make special ethnic desserts like those suggested on pages 48-50.

Agenda: Have some teens stationed by the door to greet the guests as they arrive. Other teens can sit and converse with those guests who arrive early. When all are present, choose a teen to formally welcome the guests and thank them for coming. As adult leader, offer some brief words about your youth ministry program and any other information about a specific event for which you are raising money. Allow time for pre-selected teens to briefly take turns talking about their experiences in the program or with the special projects. *Option*: Show a video that features your teens' participation. Next, call on other pre-selected teens to lead the group in the "Becoming Disciples" prayer service on pages 54-55. Make copies of the prayer service for each reader. Finally, invite the guests to eat the desserts that have been prepared. The teens can host the food and beverage table. Encourage all the teens to sit and visit personally with the guests while they are eating. End with a brief closing prayer of thanksgiving or have the group join hands and recite the Lord's Prayer.

SAMPLE   BULLETIN   ANNOUNCEMENT

Make an investment in the future of the church . . .

SHARES IN THE KINGDOM
A Fundraiser for Church Youth Ministry

What: Become a shareholder in one of the most important resources our church has to offer: OUR TEENAGERS!

Why: Over 30 church teens are raising money to go on a pilgrimage to Rome, Italy, next summer to visit the very roots and seat of our faith.

How: In order to help support our trip, become a shareholder! Contact one of the teens who is planning to go to Rome or the youth ministry office.

Cost: The cost is $15 per share. An unlimited number of shares are available!

Benefits: You will receive:
- shareholder's certificates;
- a letter from the young person while they are in Rome;
- an invitation to a bon voyage shareholder's meeting where you will be served desserts from around the world in honor of our teen pilgrims;
- a second invitation to a welcome home meeting when the teens return, including testimonials and video of their experience;
- knowledge that you helped to strengthen the future of our church

Shareholder's Certificates

I Hold a SHARE in the Kingdom	I Hold a SHARE in the Kingdom	I Hold a SHARE in the Kingdom
I Hold a SHARE in the Kingdom	I Hold a SHARE in the Kingdom	I Hold a SHARE in the Kingdom

Shareholder's Name	Shareholder's Name
Church	Church
Date	Date

Shareholder's Name	Shareholder's Name
Church	Church
Date	Date

Shareholder's Name	Shareholder's Name
Church	Church
Date	Date

SHARES IN THE KINGDOM

Record Keeping Sheet

Record the name, address, e-mail, and number of shares that each person pledges.

Name	Address	e-mail	# of Shares

Ethnic Dessert Recipes

India's Coconut Chews

This recipe will make 24 cookies.

1 c. flour	1/2 c. sugar
1/2 tsp. baking powder	2 tsp. vanilla extract
1/8 tsp. salt	3 1/2 c. sweetened, flaked coconut
2 eggs (room temp.)	

Preheat oven to 350 degrees.

Line several cookie sheets with aluminum foil and lightly butter.

In a medium-sized bowl, stir the flour, baking powder, and salt. In a large bowl using an electric mixer on high, beat the eggs and sugar for 4 to 5 minutes or until the mixture thickens and is light in color. Beat in vanilla. Using a rubber spatula, stir in the flour mixture, then fold in coconut.

Drop the dough by heaping teaspoonfuls (each cookie should contain about 2 tsp. of dough) onto prepared cookie sheets leaving about 2 inches between cookies. Bake one sheet at a time for 10 to 15 minutes or until the edges are just starting to brown.

Place cookie sheets on wire racks and let them cool for 10 minutes. Using a metal spatula, transfer the cookies to a rack and let them cool completely. When cool, seal the cookies in an airtight container.

Mexican Chocolate Cake

1 c. butter or margarine	2 c. flour
2 c. packed brown sugar	1 tsp. baking soda
2 eggs	1 1/4 c. milk
1 tsp. vanilla	
6 squares of unsweetened chocolate	

In large bowl, beat butter or margarine for 30 seconds or until light. Gradually add the brown sugar, beating until well mixed. Add eggs, one at a time, beating well after each addition. Beat in vanilla and grated chocolate (grate chocolate by freezing and then putting in food processor).

In mixing bowl, combine flour and baking soda. Add alternately with milk to beaten butter-chocolate mixture. Turn batter into greased and floured 9" x 13" pan. Bake and 350 degrees for 35 to 40 minutes. Cool and frost with premade frosting.

48

Ethnic Dessert Recipes

African Banana Peanut Cake

In a 2-quart bowl mix the following:
4 c. flour
4 tsp. baking powder
1/2 tsp. baking soda
1/4 c. cake flour
1 tsp. salt

In a 3-quart bowl cream the following:
1 1/4 c. butter or margarine   2 c. sugar

Blend in 4 eggs lightly beaten.

Fold the dry ingredients into the 3-quart bowl alternately with 8 mashed bananas and 1/2 c. coarsely chopped peanuts.

Bake in 9" x 13" baking pan at 350 degrees for 30 minutes. Test with toothpick.

Combine 1/2 c. sugar with 1 tsp. cinnamon and sprinkle cake with mixture as it comes out of the oven.

Polish Dessert Bars

2 c. flour
1/4 tsp. salt
1/2 c. sugar
1/2 c. butter
1 egg, beaten
3 tbsp. cream
1 can apple pie filling
1 jar maraschino cherries
1 c. coconut

Mix the dry ingredients. Cut butter into flour mixture with knife until crumbly. Mix beaten egg with cream and add to flour mixture. Mix lightly by hand and spread on a buttered cookie sheet.

Bake for 20 minutes at 350 degrees.

Remove quickly from oven and spread apple pie filling over crust. Bake 20 minutes longer.

When cool, decorate with maraschino cherries and coconut. Cut into small squares.

Ethnic Dessert Recipes

Hungarian Sour Cream Coffee Cake

Grease and flour a 9" or 10" tube pan.

Blend:

1 c. sugar 3 lg. eggs
1/2 c. butter (room temp.) 1 c. sour cream

Add to the above mix:

1 tsp. vanilla 2 c. flour
1 tsp. baking soda

Topping:

2/3 c. chopped pecans 1/3 c. light brown sugar

Put into tube pan. Sprinkle topping on and twirl it with a fork.

Bake 50 minutes at 350 degrees. Let cool in pan for 10 minutes. Then remove from pan and cool on rack.

Canadian Rhubarb Upside-Down Cake

Makes eight servings.

2 tbsp. butter 1/3 c. shortening
1/2 c. brown sugar 3/4 c. granulated sugar
2 c. sliced rhubarb 1 egg
1/2 c. flour 1 1/2 tsp. vanilla
2 1/2 tsp. baking powder 2/3 c. milk
1/2 tsp. salt

Melt the butter in a round baking pan. Stir in brown sugar. Arrange sliced rhubarb over mixture.

Combine flour, baking powder, and salt in a large bowl.

In a large mixing bowl, beat shortening about 30 seconds. Add sugar; beat until well combined. Add egg and vanilla; beat one minute. Add dry ingredients and milk alternately to beaten mixture, beating after each addition. Spread batter evenly over rhubarb.

Bake in a 350 degree oven for 50 to 55 minutes. Cool in pan for 5 minutes; invert onto serving plate. Serve warm.

50

Christian Hero Place Mats

Marguerite D'Youville

Marguerite was born on October 15, 1701 in Quebec, Canada. She married Francois D'Youville in 1722, and together they had three children. Marguerite was widowed in 1730 and worked very hard to support her family. While doing much charitable work, she and three friends decided to form a community of religious sisters. The Grey Nuns were established in 1745 and immediately began to serve in schools, hospitals, and orphanages. The community especially became known for its work with Eskimos. Sr. Marguerite died in 1771.

Miguel Pro

Born in Mexico in 1891, Miguel Pro loved to entertain from the time he was a child. He was a gifted actor, clown, guitarist, and singer. When Mexico fell under the rule of an atheist dictator, many priests were killed and Mass was not permitted. Miguel decided to become a Jesuit priest. He studied in Spain, California, and Nicaragua and was ordained in Belgium in 1925. Miguel decided to go back to Mexico to minister. Using disguises he was able to say Mass and care for the people while keeping the police on a constant chase. He was finally caught and executed in 1927.

CHRISTIAN HERO PLACE MATS

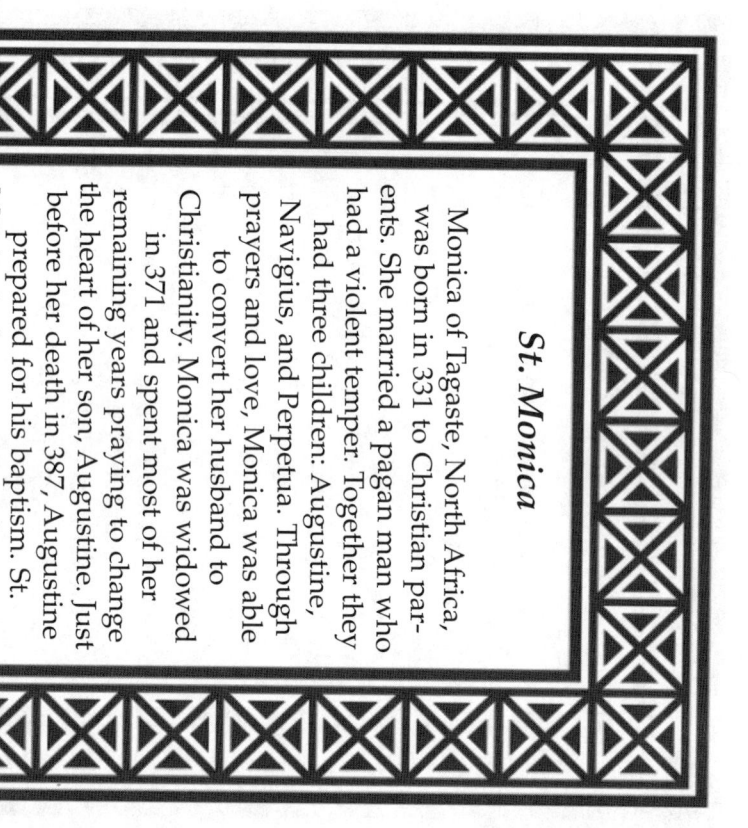

St. Monica

Monica of Tagaste, North Africa, was born in 331 to Christian parents. She married a pagan man who had a violent temper. Together they had three children: Augustine, Navigius, and Perpetua. Through prayers and love, Monica was able to convert her husband to Christianity. Monica was widowed in 371 and spent most of her remaining years praying to change the heart of her son, Augustine. Just before her death in 387, Augustine prepared for his baptism. St. Monica is the patroness of mothers and married women.

Mother Teresa

Her given name was Agnes Bojaxhiu and she was born in Yugoslavia on August 26, 1910. Though born in eastern Europe, her true home became Calcutta, India. Mother Teresa was known for her love and for the work she did with the "poorest of the poor." She began the Missionaries of Charity who today operate 600 houses for the poor in 136 countries. Mother Teresa received the Nobel Peace Prize along with admiration from countless world leaders. She died in September 1997.

Christian Hero Place Mats

St. Elizabeth of Hungary

Elizabeth was born a Hungarian princess in 1207. She married Louis of Thuringia in 1221 and the couple had four children. Elizabeth loved being a wife and mother. She was a very generous person and used her money to build hospitals to serve the needs of the sick. Her husband died six years after their marriage, and Elizabeth was forced out of her home and position by her husband's family. She then lived a life of great poverty, dedicating herself more completely to God and to the sick. Elizabeth died at age 24 in 1231. Many miracles were reported at her tomb. Pope Gregory IX canonized Elizabeth in 1235.

St. Stanislaus

St. Stanislaus, the principal patron of Poland, was born in 1031. As a "thank you" to God for this child, his noble parents guided him on a path to holiness. Stanislaus was ordained in Krakow and became an excellent preacher and beautiful example for his people. Though his people loved him, the reigning king of the time did not appreciate him. Stanislaus was continually pointing out to King Boleslaus his cruel and sinful ways. The king eventually killed Stanislaus with his own hands while he was presiding at a liturgy. Pope Innocent IV canonized St. Stanislaus in 1253. His feast day is April 11.

BECOMING DISCIPLES

Prayer Service

Consider playing a quiet instrumental piece during the prayer service as background.

Reader 1: As we gather together, we recall that it is Jesus who is the center of our admiration and hope. It is only by his perfect example of love that we and the saints who came before us learn about the joy of serving others.

Reader 2: If we were to look up the word "disciple" in the dictionary, the definition would read: "A disciple is one who learns from and spreads the teachings of another." (Pause.) It is a simple definition that when applied to Jesus has carried his message around the world for over 2,000 years. The following gospel reading asks us to be Jesus' disciples.

Proclaimer: A reading from the gospel of Matthew.

The eleven disciples went to Galilee, to the mountain to which Jesus had ordered them. When they saw him, they worshiped, but they doubted. Then Jesus approached and said to them, "All power in heaven and on earth has been given to me. Go, therefore, and make disciples of all nations, baptizing them in the name of the Father, and of the Son, and of the holy Spirit, teaching them to observe all that I have commanded you. And behold, I am with you always, until the end of the age."

The gospel of the Lord.

All: **Praise to you, Lord Jesus Christ.**

Reader 3: To be a disciple means different things to different people. The word itself means "learner," as in someone who "learns from Jesus." Take a moment and share with a person near you what you believe about the meaning of discipleship. (Pause about 90 seconds for sharing.) Over the centuries discipleship in Christ has taken many forms. Still, a true disciple is never far from Christ's command to give up on his or her desires and very life for the sake of Jesus and the gospel. Let us offer thanksgiving for all those who were not afraid of the challenges of discipleship. The response to each petition is "You were disciples of Christ."

Reader 4: To the first friends of Jesus who walked with him on earth while leaving their homes and families so that the good news might have a solid foundation, we thank you for your gift to us.

All: **You were disciples of Christ.**

Reader 5: To those inspired writers—the evangelists—who listened to God's call to record the message of Christ, we thank you for your gift to us.

All:	**You were disciples of Christ.**
Reader 6:	To those followers of Jesus who loved him at a time when it wasn't popular to be a Christian, we thank you for your gift to us.
All:	**You were disciples of Christ.**
Reader 7:	To our brothers and sisters who follow the call of the Holy Spirit and serve as missionaries to other lands and foreign cultures, we thank you for your gift to us.
All:	**You were disciples of Christ.**
Reader 8:	The gospel tells us to "observe all" that Jesus commands us. As Christians, we are blessed by the disciples in our midst—our shareholders—who have supported us in our mission to be followers of Christ. For you, we thank you for your gift to us.
All:	**You ARE disciples of Christ. Amen!**

Shares in the Kingdom Evaluation

Name _____

1. What did you learn from the shareholders while doing this fundraiser?

2. Why do you think the shareholders supported you in this fundraising effort?

3. Evaluate the shareholder's meeting(s). How were they successful? How could they be improved?

4. Define "discipleship" as you now understand it.

Candyworld

(Make, serve, and sell specialty cookies and candy while creating and playing a life-sized "Candyworld" game with younger children.)

Background

One of the most incredible things about teenagers is their ability to easily step back into the playfulness of their childhood or to journey forward to test the waters of their soon-to-be adult world.

This fundraiser, called "Candyworld," allows teens to foray into both the child and adult worlds. Young children (ages 3 and above) will be "wowed" by the attention they receive from your teens as they are led in the playing of a life-sized board game (based on the similar classic childhood board game by Milton Bradley) with cookie and candy prize treats. The adults who accompany these young children will be amazed by the creativity of your group and by all the efforts that the teens put into this project.

The Candyworld fundraiser brings to mind Jesus' words when his disciples tried to keep the children they perceived as bothersome away from him. Jesus told them point-blank, "Unless you become like children, you will not enter the kingdom of heaven." This event reminds us that when we depend on God, great things can happen!

What Is "Candyworld"?

Much like its inspiration, the Candy Land® board game, in Candyworld, young children move spaces on a game board to different "worlds" of sugary adventure. In Candyworld, however, a difference is that the players can actually win and eat candy and cookie treats from the special lands of adventure.

With colored squares set up on the floor of an auditorium or gymnasium, young children pay a small admission to roll dice and move from square to square. Specially colored pink construction paper squares are "prize squares." When the children land on these squares, the teens appear (usually dressed in special costumes) to award the lucky winners with a candy or cookie treat.

When their game is ended, the children can enjoy taking a closer look at the specially decorated spaces made to look like every child's fantasy, complete with teens costumed as clowns, kings, queens, fairies, and many other characters sure to delight the youngsters.

Finally, there are more opportunities for fundraising, as the children can take their parents to shop for more tasty homemade (by the teens) and store-bought candy and cookie treats at the concession counter, also ably supervised by the teenagers.

Getting Started

The more you are able to involve the teens in the planning and preparation of the event, the more ownership they will feel for the event itself.

If you are able to include your core group or a committee made up of youth for planning purposes, meet with them well prior to any dates you are considering for the event.

The "Candyworld Planning Meeting Agenda" (pages 58-59) provides a suggested list of items to cover as well as a short prayer service to accompany the meeting.

The "Candyworld Quickstart" (pages 60-61) provides basic and sequential information for putting on the event as well as a list of tasks that will help you get started, with or in lieu of a planning meeting.

Candyworld Planning Meeting Agenda

The following is a point-by-point meeting agenda. You can use all or some of these suggestions and arrange them to best suit your needs. You can also record decisions made at the meeting in the spaces provided.

1. Welcome
   Greet the participants. Distribute copies of the game "Names for Jesus" (page 62) for the participants to play while waiting for everyone to arrive.

2. Prayer
   Pray the prayer service, "Become Like Children" (page 63). Choose teens for the parts of leader and proclaimer. As part of this service, the teens will need to bring a photo of themselves that depicts a happy childhood memory.

3. Overview
   Share a simple description of the event (see pages 60-61 for more information).

4. Location
   Discuss where you would like to hold the Candyworld event. Record the best two suggestions.
   1.
   2.

5. Dates and Times
   Brainstorm a list of possible dates and times to hold this event. While most appropriate prior to the Christmas season, Candyworld can be adapted for use at any time of the year. Record four possible suggestions.
   1.   3.
   2.   4.

6. Decide which teens will be responsible for soliciting candy and cookie donations.
   The teens can solicit donations from merchants, family members, and parishioners. *Note*: Some candy and cookies will be packaged and sold. Other smaller items (e.g., suckers, candy kisses, etc.) will be given to the children as prizes. You will need baggies for the children to hold their prizes.

7. How many homemade candy and cookie recipes will the teens make (see pages 64-65)?
   Determine time and place for their preparation.

8. Brainstorm and record the kinds, quantities, packaging, and pricing of the cookies and candy that will be sold.

9. Making the Candyworld game
Distribute copies of the resource "Directions for Making the Candyworld Game" (page 66). Then answer the following questions:
Who will be responsible for making each part of the game?
Who will provide the materials for each part of the game?

10. Advertising (see sample bulletin announcement, page 67)
How will the event be advertised to reach more families with young children?
Who will be responsible for coordinating promotion and advertising?

11. Staffing of the event
Discuss how the game will be staffed (ticket takers, host, candy/cookie sellers, costumed characters, game guides, etc.). Write your ideas here.

12. Other issues the group counts as important
Write the ideas below.

Also, check answers for the "Names for Jesus" game distributed at the beginning of the meeting:

1. Emmanuel	2. Savior	3. Redeemer
4. Anointed One	5. King	6. Rabbi
7. Son of God	8. Prophet	9. Lord
10. Word	11. Vine	12. Bread of Life
13. Good Shepherd	14. Messiah	15. Christ

13. Closing Prayer
Say:
Lord, thank you for being with us during our time together. We pray for the success of this event. We pray for all of the young people and their families who will attend. We thank you for all of your blessings. We make this prayer in your name.

All: Amen.

CANDYWORLD QUICKSTART

The following list offers sequential planning steps and directions for the "Candyworld" event. The list also provides references to other resource material that you may use to plan for and hold the event. Try to involve the teens in as many of these steps as you can.

1. Choose the date for the Candyworld event keeping in mind the schedules of the teens and their families. If at all possible, choose a Christmas theme and schedule Candyworld for a weekend in Advent.

2. Schedule the space you will be using remembering that you will need preparation and cleanup time. Also, arrange to sell the prepared cookies and candies in an approved place outside of Sunday Mass in the weeks leading up to the event and the weekend of the event itself. This will be a great way to raise funds as well as good advertisement for the Candyworld event.

3. Decide which kinds and how much candy and cookies the teens will make. (Some recipes are included on pages 64-65.) If the preparation will be part of a regular youth ministry meeting, schedule the time and place near to the event itself. Ingredients may be solicited through donations of family members, parishioners, or local merchants.

4. Teens should also be responsible for bringing store-bought or homemade candy and cookies. *Recommendation*: Each person should bring four dozen candies and/or cookies all wrapped in packages of various quantities (3, 6, or 12). Extended family members and parishioners can be asked to donate cookies and candy as well.

5. Advertise, advertise, advertise! A sample bulletin announcement is included on page 67. Encourage one or more of your teens to design an ad to run in the local newspaper. This ad can be paid for from the profits made from the event.

6. Decide how you will price and package the candy sold separate from the playing of the game. Charge slightly more than the going rate that candy of a similar kind is sold for in retail stores. Also determine what type of packaging you will use for the candy. We collect different size coffee cans and decorate them with contact paper or wrapping paper.

7. At the place where the event will be held, reserve time for the teens to make the Candyworld game board and to decorate the room. Give a copy of the "Directions for Making the Candyworld Game" to each teen and assign them certain supplies to be responsible for. Also, call for volunteers among church and business leaders to supply more of the supplies. *Note*: Additionally, the teens who work the event should plan to dress in costume (elf, clown, prince, fairy, etc.) to further add to the fun of the occasion.

8. Displaying your bakery items in an appealing way will be important. I suggest long tables with colorful tablecloths with candy and cookies on plates or platters. You may also wish to prepackage a variety of items to sell in a convenient place after Mass.

9. The teens should wear costumes (e.g., with Christmas theme or character from the Candyworld game itself), especially when they are playing the Candyworld game with the children. At the least, the teens should wear youth group T-shirts or other clothing to distinguish themselves from the customers.

10. Familiarize yourself and the teens with how the game is played:
Four children can play this game at one time. Charge a small donation for each play. The children take turns throwing the die and moving themselves to the appropriate color. Have teens stationed at each game board prize square to award candy to children who land there. To make the game more fun, the teens should dress in appropriate costume (e.g., like a lollipop or wrapped in foil like a chocolate kiss). The child out of the group of four who finishes first wins an extra special prize (e.g., a candy bar or small gift certificate).

11. Have fun and know that each year that you hold the event it will get bigger and better. If you have any treats left over, consider making some containers for a local day care center or preschool.

12. At some point after the event, assign the participants to complete the "Candyworld Evaluation" (page 68) and return what they have written to you.

NAMES FOR JESUS

Unscramble the following words and find many of the different names or titles for Jesus. Write the names on the accompanying lines.

1. NELMEMUA _____

2. VOSIRA _____

3. EREMREDE _____

4. OTNANIDE EON _____

5. NGKI _____

6. BIBAR _____

7. NSO FO ODG _____

8. TPPHOER _____

9. DLRO _____

10. OWDR _____

11. NVEI _____

12. DRAEB FO FLEI _____

13. GODO HEEPDRHS _____

14. SSHEMIA _____

15. HSCRIT _____

BECOME LIKE CHILDREN

Prayer Service

Leader: Today we happily come together in the spirit of faith and joy in the name of our Lord, Jesus Christ. We ask God's blessing on our gathering and pray that we are successful in our endeavors. Let us begin our prayer time by sharing the photos of a happy time from our childhood. Please tell us some of the specifics about your photo and why you selected it. (Allow time for sharing.)

Proclaimer: Now, as we quiet ourselves, we pray that we can hear the Word of the Lord not only with our ears but also with our hearts. A reading from the gospel of Matthew.

At that time, the disciples approached Jesus and said, "Who is the greatest in the kingdom of heaven? He called a child over, placed it in their midst and said, "Amen, I say to you, unless you turn and become like children, you will not enter the kingdom of heaven. And whoever receives one such child as this in my name receives me.

The gospel of the Lord.

All: **Praise to you, Lord Jesus Christ.**

Leader: Reflecting on our photos, let's consider exactly what part of our own childhood God wants us to take into our adult world. (Pause.) Please share some of these qualities with a partner. (Allow time for sharing.) Now, for fun, keep passing the photos to the right until you have seen them all. (Pause until all the photos have been seen.) Thank you, Lord, for the gift of our lives. Help us to remain like children in our loving devotion to you. We ask this through Christ, our Lord.

All: **Amen.**

CANDY AND COOKIE RECIPES

Italian Christmas Cookies

2 c. sugar	2 lg. eggs
1 c. soft margarine or butter	4 c. all purpose flour
3 3/4 c. ricotta cheese	2 tsp. baking powder
2 tsp. vanilla extract	1 tsp. salt

Preheat oven to 350 degrees.

In a large bowl, mix with an automatic mixer at low speed the sugar and margarine/butter until blended. Increase speed to high; beat until light and fluffy (about 5 minutes). At medium speed, beat in ricotta, vanilla, and eggs until well combined. Reduce speed to low and add flour, baking powder, and salt; beat until dough forms.

Drop cookies 2 inches apart on an ungreased cookie sheet. Bake about 15 minutes or until lightly golden. They are a soft cookie.

When cool, frost with store-bought frosting, and decorate.

Peppermint Fudge Cookies
This recipe makes 3 dozen cookies.

8 tsp. soft margarine	1/4 c. unsweetened cocoa
1 1/4 c. brown sugar	1 1/2 c. flour
2 lg. eggs	1/4 tsp. salt
1 tsp. vanilla	1/2 tsp. baking soda

Mix together by hand the margarine, brown sugar, eggs, and vanilla in a large bowl. Sift together the cocoa, flour, salt, and soda in a separate bowl. By hand, mix together dry ingredients with margarine mixture.

Chill for 1 hour. Roll into balls, and press down lightly with a fork.

Bake at 350 degrees for 8 to 10 minutes.

Add 1 tsp. of peppermint flavoring to your favorite chocolate frosting. Frost cooled cookies.

Candy and Cookie Recipes

Grammie's Chocolate Truffles
This recipe makes about 4 dozen cookies.

3 c. semisweet chocolate chips
1 can (14 oz.) sweetened condensed milk
1 tbsp. vanilla extract
colored sprinkles or chopped nuts

In a microwave-safe bowl, heat chocolate chips and condensed milk at 50 percent power until chocolate is melted, stirring occasionally. Stir in vanilla.

Chill for 2 hours or until mixture is easy to handle. Shape into 1-inch balls. Roll in sprinkles or nuts if desired.

Fried Oyster Candy
(also known as Potato Candy)

2 large potatoes, boiled, and mashed
1 lb. powdered sugar
2 tsp. vanilla
2 c. chocolate chips, melted
16 oz. ground nuts

Mash the potatoes and let them cool. Add the powdered sugar and mix by hand. Mix in the vanilla. Drop on waxed paper or let it firm up a bit and roll into 1 inch balls. Dip in melted chocolate and roll in ground nuts. (It is interesting to watch an assembly line of teens make this candy.)

Marble Bark

4 c. semisweet chocolate chips
24 oz. white chocolate chips
20 peppermint candies or 6 candy canes unwrapped and crushed by hand or in a food processor

Spread waxed paper on a jelly roll pan or a cookie sheet with sides. Melt semisweet chocolate chips in a microwave-safe bowl. Add about half of the crushed peppermint candy. Using a spatula, swirl the chocolate mixture on waxed paper leaving some spots empty. Melt white chocolate chips and add the remaining candy. Swirl white chocolate mixture into chocolate mixture until it has the appearance of marble. Let it harden and then break it into pieces.

Directions for Making the Candyworld Game

Assign teens to make each of these components of the game. Read the game directions below to see how the various parts fit in.

Game Board Squares

Glue pieces of construction paper together to make large colored squares. These will serve as the game board squares. Make ten squares each of the primary colors: red, orange, blue, green, and yellow (total of 50 squares). Laminate if possible.

Game Board Prize Squares

Glue pieces of pink construction paper to make five squares that are the same size as the other game board squares. On the pink "prize squares" draw the following: piece of licorice, candy kiss, candy cane, lollipop, and gumdrop. Laminate if possible.

Die

Use a small, sturdy box with a lid to make the die for the game. Glue construction paper on each side of the die with one of the colors used on the game board: red, orange, blue, green, yellow, and pink.

Prize Markers

Tie some inexpensive helium balloons to ribbon and connect them with a small weight. Place a balloon by each pink square.

Prizes

Assign the teens to provide inexpensive licorice, candy kisses, candy canes, lollipops, and gumdrops as prizes. Place the prizes in baskets by the appropriate squares. Provide small baggies for the "winners" to put their prizes in.

Game Set Up

Alternate colored squares on the floor of the gym or auditorium. Place the prize squares (and balloons) at regular intervals in between the primary colors. Also keep the appropriate prizes near the prize squares.

Playing the Game

Review the directions for playing the game and determine tasks teens will take to help play the game.

Four children can play this game at one time. Charge a small donation for each play. The children take turns throwing the die and moving themselves to the appropriate color. Have teens stationed at each game board prize square to award candy to children who land there. To make the game more fun, the teens should dress in appropriate costume (e.g., like a lollipop or wrapped in foil like a chocolate kiss). The child out of the group of four who finishes first wins an extra special prize (e.g., a candy bar or small gift certificate).

Sample Bulletin Announcement

The Holy Name Youth Group Proudly Presents

CANDYWORLD!

What: Children will enjoy playing a full-sized board game with candy and cookie prizes to the winners while adults shop for favorite candy and cookie items such as caramels, truffles, turtles, spritz, and divinity fudge.

When: Saturday, December 2 from 4:00 p.m. to 6:00 p.m.
Sunday, December 3 from 8:00 a.m. to 1:00 p.m.

Where: The Candyworld game is played in the church auditorium. Candy and cookies will also be sold outside of church after Mass on both Saturday and Sunday.

Why: The Holy Name Youth Group is raising funds to pay for our trip to World Youth Day in Toronto, Canada.

How: We will be selling different sized packages of candy and cookies. The children will play a real-life board game where they can win candy and cookie prizes. Cost for each child to play the game is $3.

CANDYWORLD EVALUATION

Name _____

1. Which task(s) were you responsible for in this fundraiser? How do you rate your effort and performance?

2. How could this fundraiser be improved?

3. What did you learn about yourself by participating in "Candyworld"?

4. Tell about some personal contact you had with a customer (adult or child) that was inspiring to you.

The Storyteller

(Teens produce and act-out simple dramas of their favorite children's stories and invite guests, from young children to older adults, to attend.)

Background

We all know that Jesus was a great storyteller. Sometimes I close my eyes and pretend that I am in the crowd as Jesus tells one of his famous parables. I can imagine how the charisma of this itinerant preacher comes through with each sentence. Everyone listens with great interest to his stories, hoping to find a pearl of wisdom and to discover more about Jesus. Imaginations are surely great.

The tradition of storytelling in Jesus' time was a method used to both pass on history and also to share a greater value and lesson for life. Those who heard Jesus' parables were given a method to pass on his message to others. Today, this technique still applies. Homilists, for example, often begin their homilies with a story. Our long-standing oral tradition is a direct path to our imaginations.

What Is "The Storyteller"?

This fundraiser basically involves teens presenting children's stories in dramatic fashion, inviting children with their parents and grandparents to attend, and charging those who attend a small donation (e.g., $3 per person or $7 per family).

There are three basic methods that can be used to tell the stories.

In the first, one person tells the story in a dramatic way while taking on the character roles as they appear in the story. Other teens can provide props and background sound effects or serve as silent extras.

In a second method, one person reads the narrator portions of the story. Other teens speak the conversational lines of the other characters. Appropriate props are needed in this method as well.

A third method has a teen read a children's story off-stage while other teens mime the story.

Think for a moment about the teens you work with. Who are young people with personalities just screaming for the spotlight? These teens probably come to mind very easily and would benefit from being "the stars" for this occasion.

Many other blessings come from The Storyteller fundraiser. This event is an opportunity for young children, parents, grandparents, and other significant adults in the church community to be together in a Christian environment while witnessing the outstanding talents of the teens.

Don't be surprised if after their performances your teens are asked to tell their stories again at other church functions.

Getting Started

The main features of this fundraiser are the stories and those who tell them. This event is well-suited for teens to help in the planning. A planning meeting agenda is included on pages 71-72.

Invite the teens to bring samples of their favorite children's stories, tales, and parables to a planning meeting. This time together can also serve as a "tryout" and rehearsal for the event itself. Some opportunity for rehearsal is absolutely necessary.

Make sure to come to agreement on cost for admission as well as overall theme of the event.

For additional planning suggestions consult "The Storyteller Quickstart" (page 73).

The Storyteller Planning Meeting Agenda

The following is a point-by-point meeting agenda. You can use all or some of these suggestions and arrange them to best suit your needs. You can also record decisions made at the meeting in the spaces provided.

Make sure the teens know to bring a favorite children's story (preferably one with a positive lesson) to the meeting.

1. Welcome
Greet the participants as they arrive. Provide some light snacks and beverages for the teens to share while waiting for everyone to arrive.

2. Overview
Explain the fundraiser. Share an example of a children's story appropriate for this event. Ask the teens to share the children's story they have brought. Ask them to tell why they like it and what lesson they learned from it.

3. Prayer
Distribute copies of "The Lord's Generosity" prayer service (pages 74-75) to all the teens and pray this service with the group.

4. Dates and Times
List four possible suggestions for when to hold the event. If you choose a certain theme for all the stories (e.g., Christmas or Easter), that will affect the date chosen.
1.
2.
3.
4.

5. Programming
Determine how many stories will be read based on the number of participants and an expected 45 to 60 minute time frame.

6. Choose Stories
Based on the presentations of the stories brought in by teens and of others you know of (see pages 76-77 for ideas), choose the stories that will be part of the event.

7. Method of Storytelling
Determine which methods of storytelling will be used (see page 69 under "Getting Started"). If possible, audition the teens for roles at this time. Also determine an additional date for the teens to meet for a final rehearsal.

8. Advertising (see sample bulletin announcement, page 78)
How will the event be advertised to reach more families with young children?

Who will be responsible for coordinating promotion and advertising?

9. Food for the Event
Will you host a light food and beverage table?

Who will be responsible for food and ancillary items?

10. Other Decisions
Recruit an audiovisual crew to be responsible for lighting and sound.
Who are some adults who may be adept at storytelling or who are well-known in the church (pastor, teacher, parents, coach, etc.)? Ask some of these people to sign up for guest appearances as storytellers.

Determine who will be the master or mistress of ceremonies.

11. Closing Prayer
Stand and recite together an Our Father or Hail Mary.

The Storyteller Quickstart

The following list offers sequential planning steps and directions for "The Storyteller" event. The list also provides references to other resource materials that you may use to plan for and hold the event. Try to involve the teens in as many of these steps as you can.

1. Using your school and church calendars as a guide, select a season and date for "The Storyteller" event. Reserve a space, keeping in mind that a social will also be part of the festivities. *Optional*: Plan for a microphone and spotlight to enhance the presentation.

2. Choose stories to be enacted that are age-appropriate to children and families. See the list of suggestions on pages 76-77. Also, refer to the library for other popular selections of children's stories.

3. Gather interested teens for a planning meeting (see pages 71-72) and/or rehearsal.

4. Assign roles (including storytellers, actors, master/mistress of ceremony, hospitality chairs, etc.). Practice the storytelling program until it takes on real professionalism and you are comfortable with the final production. *Optional*: Follow the sample program for "The Storyteller" event listed below. This particular event is organized with an Advent/Christmas theme.
    A. Welcome by the master/mistress of ceremonies
    B. A reading from Luke 1:26-38 by the MC
    C. *Why Christmas Trees Aren't Perfect* Introduction and Presentation
    D. A reading from Luke 1:39-45 by the MC
    E. *The Christmas Miracle of Jonathan Toomey* Introduction and Presentation
    F. A reading from Luke 2:1-14 by the MC
    G. *Gloria, the Christmas Angel* Introduction and Presentation
    H. A reading from Luke 2:15-20 by the MC
    I. *A Night the Stars Danced for Joy* Introduction and Presentation
    J. Final words of thanks from the MC
    K. Food and beverage social

5. Advertise the event in the church bulletin and, if possible, in local newspapers. A sample bulletin announcement is included on page 78.

6. At a youth meeting after the fundraiser, distribute to the teens "The Storyteller Evaluation" (page 79). Use the questions as a basis for discussion.

The Lord's Generosity

Prayer Service
Choose for the "storyteller" role someone adept at sharing a good story.

Leader: Jesus was called "rabbi," which means "teacher," when he walked the earth because his words often changed the minds and hearts of those who listened to him. Though Jesus did not invent parables, he used them as a method of teaching by allowing his listeners to compare themselves to the characters in the story. Today Jesus' words still inspire us to evaluate and reform our lives. Please listen carefully to his words.

Proclaimer: A reading from the gospel of Matthew.

"The kingdom of heaven is like a landowner who went out at dawn to hire laborers for his vineyard. After agreeing with them for the usual daily wage, he sent them into his vineyard. Going out about nine o'clock, he saw others standing idle in the marketplace, and he said to them, 'You too go into my vineyard, and I will give you what is just.' So they went off. [And] he went out again around noon, and around three o'clock, and did likewise. Going out about five o'clock, he found others standing around, and said to them, 'Why do you stand here idle all day?' They answered, 'Because no one has hired us.' He said to them, 'You too go into my vineyard.' When it was evening the owner of the vineyard said to his foreman, 'Summon the laborers and give them their pay, beginning with the last and ending with the first.' When those who had started about five o'clock came, each received the usual daily wage. So when the first came, they thought that they would receive more, but each of them also got the usual wage. And on receiving it they grumbled against the landowner, saying, 'These last ones worked only one hour, and you have made them equal to us, who bore the day's burden and heat.' He said to one of them in reply, 'My friend, I am not cheating you. Did you not agree with me for the usual daily wage? Take what is yours and go. What if I wish to give this last one the same as you? [Or] am I not free to do as I wish with my own money? Are you envious because I am generous?' Thus, the last will be first, and the first will be last."

The gospel of the Lord.

All: **Praise to you, Lord Jesus Christ.**

Leader: Reflect for a moment on the meaning of the parable for your life. (Pause.) Now, please listen to the story "An Afternoon in the Park."

The storyteller shares the story "An Afternoon in the Park" in his or her own words.

Storyteller: "An Afternoon in the Park"
There was once a little boy who wanted to meet God. He knew it was a long trip to where God lived, so he packed his suitcase with cookies and a six-pack of root beer.

When he had gone about three blocks, he met a woman. She was sitting in the park just staring at some pigeons. The boy sat down next to her and opened his suitcase. He was about to take a drink from his root beer when he noticed that the lady looked hungry. So he offered her a cookie. She gratefully accepted it and smiled at him. Her smile was so pretty that the boy wanted to see it again. So he offered her a root beer. Once again she smiled at him. The boy was delighted.

They sat there all afternoon eating and smiling at one another. But they never said a word.

As it grew dark, the boy realized how tired he was and he got up to leave. But before he had gone more than a few steps, he turned around, ran back to the old woman, and gave her a hug. She gave him her biggest smile ever.

When the boy opened the door to his own house a short time later, his mother was surprised by the look of joy on his face.

She asked him, "What did you do today that made you so happy?"

He replied, "I had lunch with God." But before his mother could respond, he added, "You know what? God has the most beautiful smile I have ever seen."

Meanwhile, the boy asked his mom what she did all day. His mother told him:

"I ate cookies and drank root beer in the park with God."

(Adapted from a story by Julie A. Manhan. Reprinted with permission.)

Leader: How did the mom and son find God? (Allow responses.) How do you find God in others? (Allow responses.)

We pray for the success of this fundraiser and our planning time together. Bless us and keep us in your care. We ask this in your name.

All: **Amen.**

The Storyteller

Book and Story Recommendations

Advent/Christmas
The Christmas Miracle of Jonathon Toomey by Susan Wojciechowski (Tommy Nelson, 1998).
Gloria, the Christmas Angel by Scott Anthony Asalone and Gerard A. Pottebaum, eds. (Treehaus Communications, 2000).
Jacob's Gift by Max Lucado and Robert Hunt (Tommy Nelson, Inc., 1998).
The Legend of the Christmas Rose by William Hooks (HarperCollins, 1999).
A Night the Stars Danced for Joy by Bob Hartman (Lion Publishing, 1999).
Three Wise Women by Mary Hoffman and Lynn Russell (Phyllis Fogelman Books, 1999).
Why Christmas Trees Aren't Perfect by Richard H. Schneider (Abingdon Press, 1987).

Lent/Easter
A Tale of Chicken Sunday by Patricia Polacco (Philomel Books, 1992).
The Easter Angels by Bob Hartman (Chariot Victor Publishing, 1999).
The Gift by Robert F. Morneau and Marjorie Mau (Kodomdo Press, 1995).
Three Trees by Angela Elwell Hunt (Chariot Victor Publishing, 1989).

Generosity/Love
All You Ever Need by Max Lucado (Crossway Books, 2000).
The Quiltmaker's Gift by Jeff Brumbeau (Scholastic Trade, 2001).
A Tale From Paleface Creek by Robert F. Morneau (Paulist Press, 2000).
Wilfrid Gordon McDonald Partridge by Mem Fox (Kane Miller Book Publishers, 1989).

Integrity/Forgiveness
The Broken Promise by Ravi K. Zacharias and Lad Odell (Chariot Victor Publishing, 2000).

Miracles of Love
The Acrobat and the Angel by Mark Shannon (Putnam Publishing Group, 1999).

The Presence of God
Places of Power by Michael DeMunn (Dawn Publications, 1997).

Generations of Faith
The Keeping Quilt by Patricia Polacco (Simon and Shuster, 1998).

Sample Bulletin Announcement

Grandparents, grandchildren, and everyone else young at heart, in honor of Jesus the Storyteller, please join us for our annual presentation of

THE STORYTELLER

What: A dynamic presentation of stories specially selected for Advent and Christmas as told by your church teenagers. Refreshments will be served following the presentation.

Who: This presentation is intended for anyone who wants to get into the Christmas spirit.

When: Sunday, December 10 from 2:30 to 3:30 p.m.

Where: The presentation will take place in the church hall with the refreshment reception to follow in the foyer.

Why: Our church youth are raising money for the local shelter for domestic violence. All proceeds will be donated to that agency.

Cost: The cost is $3 per person or $7 per family. No reservations are necessary.

If you are a teenager and would like to participate in this event, please call the Youth Ministry office.

THE STORYTELLER EVALUATION

Name _____

1. What was your role in this fundraiser?

2. How was this fundraiser successful? What can be done to improve this fundraiser in the future?

3. What new thing did you learn about yourself or others by participating in "The Storyteller"?

4. Share one or more comments you heard from someone who attended this fundraiser.

THE BREAD BASKET

(Teens bake different kinds of breads and sell them at their church or at local businesses or community events.)

Background

One of the questions I always enjoy asking children who are preparing for First Communion is "Why do you think Jesus chose something as simple as bread to be the way in which he is really present to us?" After a short pause, the hands start waving and the children are ready to respond.

"Because everybody likes bread," offers the first child.

"Because everybody can afford bread," responds another.

"Because bread tastes good and fills us up so we won't be hungry," the third states.

Jesus truly knew what he was doing when he chose ordinary bread as the way to remain with us.

On another level, making and sharing bread also points to the idea of community participation and celebration. The teens who participate in The Bread Basket fundraiser will enjoy the time they spend together making and wrapping the breads and also sharing their own family recipes and stories. By attaching scripture passages with references to bread on the packages, they will be doing their part to spread the good news of Jesus.

What Is "The Bread Basket"?

For The Bread Basket fundraiser teens gather ingredients and work with experienced parishioners to prepare homemade bread to be sold for a profit. The homemade bread is sold at the church following Sunday Masses. The bread might also be sold at local businesses and through meetings of local organizations like the Knights of Columbus.

In addition, in the planning and execution of the event, teens come to appreciate the ongoing Christian fellowship that arises in the baking and sharing of bread. A prayer service that accompanies a planning meeting helps to this end. Also, as part of the packaging and selling of the bread, the teens attach a scripture passage to the wrapping to further help to spread the good news of Christ.

Getting Started

A planning meeting agenda for "The Bread Basket" fundraiser is included on pages 82-83. A meeting of this kind will help the teens be involved in the decisions leading up to the baking and selling of the breads.

However, a youth minister or other adult leader can make many of the decisions involved in this fundraiser on his or her own. In this case, "The Bread Basket Quickstart" (page 84) can help with this process.

The Bread Basket Planning Meeting Agenda

The following is a point-by-point meeting agenda. You can use all or some of these suggestions and arrange them to best suit your needs. You can also record decisions made at the meeting in the spaces provided.

1. Welcome

Greet the participants. Plan to have some homemade or other specialty breads on hand for the teens to share as they arrive.

2. Prayer

Pray the prayer service "In the Breaking of the Bread" (page 85) with the teens. Make copies of the resource for teens serving as leader and proclaimer.

3. Overview

Share a brief overview of the fundraiser with the teens. See "The Bread Basket Quickstart" (page 84) and "The Bread Basket Baking Day Agenda" (page 86) for more information

4. Dates and Times

Brainstorm a list of dates and times for holding the fundraiser. Remember that the days for baking and selling the bread should be held in close proximity. Record the four best suggestions here.
1.
2.
3.
4.

5. Discuss and record answers to the following questions:

Who will supply the baking utensils (pans, bowls, etc.)?

How will we get the ingredients to make the breads?

Where will we bake the bread?

Who are special bakers in the church who might help us with the baking?

What recipes will we use? (See pages 88-89 for more ideas.)

Where and when will we sell the bread?

How much will we charge for the loaves?

What type of materials do we need for the sale day (e.g., tables, signs, money box)?

Which teens will participate in the various parts of this event from preparation to selling to cleanup?

6. Advertising (see sample bulletin announcement, page 92)
   Who will be responsible for coordinating promotion and advertising?

7. Closing Prayer
   Stand, join hands, and pray an Our Father to conclude the meeting.

The Bread Basket Quickstart

The following list offers sequential planning steps and directions for "The Bread Basket" event. The list also provides references to other resource material that you may use to plan for and hold the event. Try to involve the teens in as many of these steps as you can.

1. Using your school and church calendars as a guide, select a weekend that will be good for teens and their parents (i.e., avoid "big game" or "dance" weekends). For example, Friday evening can be reserved as baking time and Saturday and Sunday for sales. Make sure to arrange to be able to sell the bread after Sunday Masses as well.

2. Contact local businesses to see if you might be able to set up a table in the entryway of their store to sell bread. If you have a large group, find at least four locations.

3. Schedule the church or school kitchen for baking day. Determine which baking utensils will need to be supplied by the teens.

4. Contact local grocery stores for donations of the basic ingredients for the breads such as eggs, flour, sugar, and oil, as well as plastic wrap and curling ribbon for packaging. Also, put an announcement in the Sunday bulletin suggesting what you need and asking parishioners to volunteer the needed items.

5. Determine what types of breads the teens would like to make. Use some or all of the recipes included on pages 88-89. Plan to bake a wide variety of bread types. Make sure to have more than enough ingredients available.

6. Advertise in the Sunday bulletin for donations of bread made at home by parishioners. These too can be sold. Also, recruit a "master baker" to help with the bread baking day.

7. Advertise the event itself at various locations. A sample bulletin announcement is included on page 92.

8. On the day the breads are to be prepared, follow "The Bread Basket Baking Day Agenda" (page 86).

9. Set up a schedule for the times and places the teenagers will be selling their breads. Be sure to include an adult chaperone for each crew of teens. Also make sure the teens have items like a tablecloth, table, signs, napkins, and money box for each selling location.

10. At a future meeting of the fundraiser participants, pass out "The Bread Basket Evaluation" and have them complete it and return it to you.

In the Breaking of the Bread

Prayer Service
Make copies of this resource for the leader and the proclaimer.

Leader: Let us offer our prayer in the name of Jesus, our Lord and Savior. (Pause.) Though we are together to plan a fundraiser, let us also take time to appreciate each other and our time together. We are grateful for the presence of the Lord in our midst. The focus of our fundraiser is bread so let us listen to one of the many gospel passages that speak of bread in connection with the presence of Jesus.

Proclaimer: A reading from the gospel of Luke.

Now that very day two of them were going to a village seven miles from Jerusalem called Emmaus, and they were conversing about all the things that had occurred. And it happened that while they were conversing and debating, Jesus himself drew near and walked with them, but their eyes were prevented from recognizing him. . . . As they approached the village to which they were going, he gave the impression that he was going on farther. But they urged him, "Stay with us, for it is nearly evening and the day is almost over." So he went in to stay with them. And it happened that, while he was with them at table, he took bread, said the blessing, broke it, and gave it to them. With that their eyes were opened and they recognized him, but he vanished from their sight.

The gospel of the Lord.

All: **Praise to you, Lord Jesus Christ.**

Leader: Take some time to share with another the significance of a family bread recipe or a time when you have experienced God's presence when you shared bread. (Allow time for discussion.) Let us pray. Creator God, we thank you for the gift of ordinary bread. With this simple food, you not only have nourished our bodies but also our spirits. By the gift of your Son to the world, we will never be hungry. For this and all your gifts to us, we thank you.

All: **Amen.**

BREAD BASKET BAKING DAY AGENDA

Begin early, allowing enough time for the preparation and baking of the bread.

1. Prepare the various work stations necessary for bread baking ahead of time. The number of stations will depend on the number of participants.

2. If you are also collecting ingredients for the breads, have a table set up that is easily accessible for them to be dropped off at.

3. Baking pans should be many different sizes and can be brought by the teens. Inexpensive aluminum pans can also be purchased and used for the baking.

4. Make copies of any of the bread recipes found on pages 88-89 to have available for all of the participants.

5. Allow the teens to mix the ingredients and bake the breads, being careful to make notations of the names of the particular breads by identifying them on each pan.

6. As the bread cools, prepare a wrapping and marking table. The table should be supplied with plastic wrap, copies of the scripture passages with scissors to cut them apart (see pages 90-91), a hole punch, curling ribbon, and pens. Have the teens wrap the breads and tie with curling ribbons that have a scripture passage attached. On the blank side of the scripture passage, have them print the name of the bread and its cost.

7. Have the teens make signs for the sales tables that include the name of the youth group, why you are having the sale, and of course the cost of the breads. *Optional*: Have the group prepare table centerpieces from bread dinner rolls. Directions for making the centerpieces are on page 87.

8. Don't forget to have the teens clean up the preparation area before moving on to the sales area.

Directions for Making Bread Basket Centerpiece

Materials Needed:
cooking spray
2 cookie sheets
24 frozen dinner rolls
plastic wrap
1 small ovenproof bowl (about 1 1/2 quarts, 4-5 inches tall, and 6 inches wide)
1 large egg

Directions:
1. Lightly spray one cookie sheet and place the frozen dinner rolls on the sheet.
2. Lightly spray plastic wrap before using it to cover the rolls.
3. Allow the rolls to rise for about four hours.
4. Lightly spray the second cookie sheet.
5. Invert the bowl on the second cookie sheet and spray lightly.
6. Once the rolls have risen, set aside 13 rolls for rolling into 9-inch "ropes." Then flatten each rope into 3/4 inch wide strips.
7. Taking the 13 strips, gently press one end to the middle of the bowl top, letting the rope drape down the side onto baking sheets. Evenly place each strip.

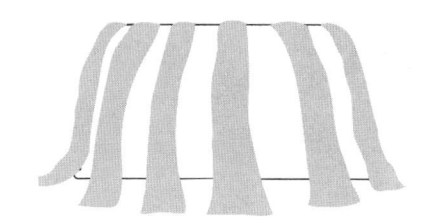

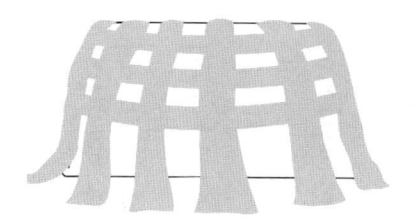

8. Take three dinner rolls at once, roll then into a ball, and then into an 18-inch rope. Do not flatten.
9. Starting at the top edge of the bowl, weave the rope over/under the flat strips, turning the cookie sheet as you go.
10. Roll three more dinner rolls into an 18-inch rope and attach to the end of the first rope.
11. Continue weaving to cover the bowl. Tuck in the end of the last rope. Trim any ropes that rest on the cookie sheet.
12. Beat one large egg and use it to "brush" the basket. This is the glaze that will make your basket shiny.
13. Preheat the oven to 350 degrees. Bake 10 minutes and then turn the cookie sheet 180 degrees and bake for another 15 minutes or until golden brown.
14. Using oven mitts, carefully invert the basket onto a cookie sheet, gently pressing down to flatten the bottom. Return the basket to shut-off oven for another 30 minutes.
15. Transfer the basket to a wire rack; let cool for 15 minutes. Gently twist the bowl to disengage it from the basket. Let cool.

Bread Recipes

Pistachio Bread

1 pkg. yellow cake mix	1/4 c. water
1 pkg. pistachio pudding mix	green food coloring
	2 tbsp. sugar
4 eggs, beaten	2 tbsp. cinnamon
1 c. sour cream	
1/4 c. oil	

Combine cake mix, pudding mix, eggs, sour cream, oil, and water in a large bowl. Add green food coloring until the shade desired. Mix together sugar and cinnamon in a separate small bowl.

Grease two regular bread pans or 4 smaller pans. Fill pans half way. Top with cinnamon mixture, then the rest of the batter.

Bake at 350 degrees for 40 minutes.

Eggnog Bread

1/4 c. butter or margarine, melted	1 tsp. salt
	1 c. eggnog
3/4 c. sugar	1/2 c. chopped pecans
2 eggs, beaten	1/2 c. raisins
2 1/4 c. flour	1/2 c. chopped red and green candied cherries
2 tsp. baking powder	

In a large bowl, mix well the butter, sugar, and eggs. In a separate bowl, combine flour, baking powder, and salt. Mix dry ingredients into butter mixture alternating with eggnog. Fold in pecans, raisins, and cherries. Spoon into two greased mini-loaf pans. Bake at 350 degrees for 40 minutes.

Poppy Seed Bread

1 pkg. lemon cake mix	1/4 c. hot water
1 pkg. instant vanilla pudding mix	1/2 c. oil
	1/2 c. nuts
1/4 c. poppy seeds	4 eggs, beaten

Mix all the ingredients together. Add mixture to two greased regular bread pans or four small pans.

Bake at 350 degrees for 45 minutes.

Bread Recipes

Pumpkin Pecan Loaves

3 1/3 c. flour
3 c. sugar
2 tsp. baking soda
1 1/2 tsp. salt
1 tsp. cinnamon
1 tsp. nutmeg
2/3 c. water
1 c. oil
4 eggs lightly beaten
15 oz. can of solid packed pumpkin
1/2 c. chopped pecans

Glaze:
1/4 c. butter or margarine
1/4 c. granulated sugar
1/4 c. packed brown sugar
1/4 c. whipping cream
2/3 c. powdered sugar
1 tsp. vanilla extract

In a bowl, combine flour, sugar, soda, salt, cinnamon, and nutmeg. Combine the water, oil, eggs, and pumpkin. Mix well. Stir into dry ingredients until just combined; fold in pecans. Spoon into 4 greased mini-loaf pans.

Bake at 350 degrees for 60 to 65 minutes or until a toothpick inserted near the center comes out clean. Cool for 10 minutes before removing from pans to wire rack.

For glaze, combine the butter, granulated and brown sugars, and cream in a saucepan. Cook on low heat until sugar is dissolved, stirring constantly. Cool for twenty minutes. Stir in the powdered sugar and vanilla until smooth. Drizzle over cooled loaves.

Honey Spice Bread

1/3 c. milk
2/3 c. packed brown sugar
2 c. flour
2 tsp. baking powder
1/2 tsp. cinnamon
1 1/2 tsp. nutmeg
1/8 tsp. cloves
1/2 c. honey
2 eggs, beaten
1/3 c. oil

Glaze:
1/3 c. powdered sugar 1 to 2 tsp. milk
candied fruit

In medium saucepan combine milk and brown sugar. Cook and stir over low heat until sugar is dissolved.

In bowl, stir together flour, baking powder, cinnamon, nutmeg, and cloves. Gradually blend together the milk mixture, the flour mixture, honey, eggs, and oil. Turn batter into two greased and floured mini-loaf pans.

Bake at 350 degrees for 55 to 60 minutes or until done, covering with foil the last 15 minutes. Cool in pan for 10 minutes. Remove from pan and cool thoroughly.

Combine powdered sugar and milk to frost the cooled loaves. Decorate with candied fruit.

Scripture Passages

Cut apart the gospel passages below and attach to the packaged bread with curling ribbon. Print the name and cost of the bread on the reverse side.

Then the two recounted what had taken place on the way and how he was made known to them in the breaking of the bread.
—*Luke 24:35*

So Jesus said to them, "Amen, amen, I say to you, it was not Moses who gave the bread from heaven; my Father gives you the true bread from heaven."
—*John 6:32*

"For the bread of God is that which comes down from heaven and gives life to the world."
—*John 6:33*

They devoted themselves to the teaching of the apostles and to the communal life, to the breaking of the bread and to the prayers.
—*Acts 2:42*

Because the loaf of bread is one, we, though many, are one body, for we all partake of the one loaf.
—*1 Corinthians 10:17*

He said in reply, "It is written: 'One does not live by bread alone, but by every word that comes forth from the mouth of God.'"
—*Matthew 4:4*

Then he took the bread, said the blessing, broke it, and gave it to them, saying, "This is my body, which will be given for you; do this in memory of me."
—*Luke 22:19*

Jesus said to them, "I am the bread of life; whoever comes to me will never hunger, and whoever believes in me will never thirst."
—*John 6:35*

Which one of you would hand his son a stone when he asks for a loaf of bread, or a snake when he asks for a fish?
—*Matthew 7:9-10*

Sample Bulletin Announcement

Break bread and share fellowship with
the Holy Name Youth Group as it presents

THE BREAD BASKET

What: Teenagers and other special bakers from our church have prepared several delicious homemade specialty breads for you to purchase and enjoy.

When: The sale will take place after all Masses on November 21 and 22. The bread will also be on sale all week at specially marked tables outside of Beeman's Cleaners from 3:30 to 5 p.m.

Why: The Holy Name Youth Group is raising funds to pay for a trip to Washington, D.C., in January to participate in the annual Right to Life march.

How: Many kinds of bread are available with prices ranging from $5 to $7.

The Bread Basket Evaluation

Name _____

1. How did you participate in The Bread Basket fundraiser?

2. Rate the success of this fundraiser in terms of:

    money raised

    improving your relationship with God

    building community among your peers

3. What could make this fundraiser even better if held again?

4. Tell how you witnessed God's blessing on the group during the time this fundraiser was held.

Strike Up the Band

(Various musical groups from your local high schools such as bands, choirs, drill teams, and rock and roll groups come to the church for a special performance attended by the local community.)

Background

A fundraiser that accents the musical talents of teenagers is often an apt event for late in the school calendar as music itself helps provide glimpses of the resurrection and allows for teens to "clap their hands" and "shout to God with joyful cries" (see Psalm 47:2).

Many teens have been taking music lessons for years. Often this talent is hidden from all but their most intimate friends. Search out teens talented in performing arts, ask them to practice and play for your fundraiser, and secure other teens to work diligently to make sure all the friends, family members, and parishioners possible are invited to attend to offer their moral and financial support.

What Is "Strike Up the Band"?

Strike Up the Band is the opportunity for local teens to use their music and dance abilities for the enjoyment of others and for the benefit of your fundraising efforts. Extend an invitation to local band directors, dance instructors, and drill coaches to invite local teens to put on a performance you can advertise and invite your church to attend. Also, consider inviting local teens who have formed their own musical groups outside of school to perform in a separate concert or "battle of the bands" with the intended audience being the teens themselves.

A feature of this fundraiser is the diversity of the patrons. Parents and grandparents will definitely want to be in the audience as their teens show off their many gifts. Interested families with younger children will turn out for enjoyment and to support a worthy cause.

As you plan this event, think about all of the many possibilities for dates, locations, and participants. Be a dreamer and envision how you would like the project to turn out. Then work for that goal. Sometimes just a few phone calls will reap wonderful possibilities to make this fundraiser one of your most successful.

Getting Started

A planning meeting agenda for "Strike Up the Band" is included on pages 96-97. A meeting for this fundraiser is especially beneficial as the teens will be able to suggest bands and other performing arts groups that may be appropriate for this event.

The "Strike Up the Band Quickstart" on page 98 provides helpful hints for youth ministers and other adult leaders with or in lieu of a planning meeting.

Strike Up the Band Planning Meeting Agenda

The following is a point-by-point meeting agenda. You can use all or some of these suggestions and arrange them to best suit your needs. You can also record decisions made at the meeting in the spaces provided.

1. Welcome

Play some popular music on a CD player as the teens arrive. Provide some light snacks as well.

2. Prayer

Prepare a leader and proclaimer for the prayer service, "Rejoice in the Lord" (page 99). Pass out copies of the resource to both the leader and proclaimer and have them lead the prayer with the rest of the group.

3. Overview

Explain in general terms the fundraiser: teenage music, dance, and other performing arts groups participate in a public performance. The admission charged to the event is the basis for raising funds.

4. Possible Performers

Ask the teens to brainstorm music groups and individuals who might be willing to perform at this event. Write as many suggestions as you can in the space below.

1. 6.
2. 7.
3. 8.
4. 9.
5. 10.

5. Date and Time

List some possible dates and times, making sure to choose a weekend where there are not many conflicts with other teen and family events.

6. Location

Where will the event be held?

7. Cost

How much will be charged for admission?

8. Program

Will you produce and sell a program? Who will be responsible for writing and producing the program? Who will sell the program?

9. Social

Discuss ideas for selling or offering free refreshments following the performance.

10. Master/Mistress of Ceremonies
   Brainstorm a list of candidates.

11. Advertising
   How can the event be publicized? (See the sample bulletin announcement, page 100).

12. Closing Prayer
   Pray:
   Lord, bless the talents of those who will perform in our performing arts fundraiser. Thank you for the special gifts you have given to all of us. We ask this in your name.

   All: Amen.

Strike Up the Band Quickstart

The following list offers sequential planning steps and directions for the "Strike Up the Band" event. The list also provides references to other resource material that you may use to plan for and hold the event. Try to involve the teens in as many of these steps as you can.

1. This event works well as a spring concert. However, if schools are holding the same type of event, you may want to consider choosing an alternate date.

2. Reserve a large auditorium or hall for the concert. If you have chosen the concert for a warm weather month, you may also consider holding it outdoors.

3. Invite up to five musical or performing arts groups to perform. Contact local high school performing arts departments and tap into suggestions offered by your teens.

4. Assign a group of teens to handle advertising for the event. Have them design and print flyers that can be distributed at local schools, theaters, churches, and libraries. Call local newspapers and radio stations to inquire if they will make a public service announcement for your event. Also advertise in your church bulletin (see sample bulletin insert on page 100).

5. Assign a group of teens to write, design, and have printed a program for the event. The program can have not only the order of performance, but also names and background information on the groups that are performing.

6. Recruit teens to serve as hospitality helpers at the concert, perhaps selling refreshments as well as taking donations for admission and distributing programs.

7. Recruit an energetic teen to serve as mistress or master of ceremonies. If the person has comedic skills, this might be the chance to put those to use by telling jokes or short stories in between each performance.

8. If the music groups will need help with audio-visual needs (e.g., lighting, microphone, speakers, etc.), also recruit a team of teens to help in this area.

9. The concert should last anywhere between 90 minutes to two hours.

10. Enjoy the performance.

11. At a future youth meeting, pass out the "Strike Up the Band Evaluation," have the participants complete it and return it to you.

REJOICE IN THE LORD

Prayer Service

Leader: We gather today to praise the Lord and to plan an event which will be a witness to God's love. We ask you, Lord, to be with us in this planning and for the wisdom to do your will. Open our ears to your word and let it inspire us. We ask this in your name.

All: **Amen.**

Proclaimer: A reading from the gospel of Mark.

When the sabbath was over, Mary Magdalene, Mary, the mother of James, and Salome bought spices so that they might go and anoint him. Very early when the sun had risen, on the first day of the week, they came to the tomb. They were saying to one another, "Who will roll back the stone for us from the entrance to the tomb?" When they looked up, they saw that the stone had been rolled back; it was very large. On entering the tomb they saw a young man sitting on the right side, clothed in a white robe, and they were utterly amazed. He said to them, "Do not be amazed! You seek Jesus of Nazareth, the crucified. He has been raised; he is not here. Behold the place where they laid him. But go and tell his disciples and Peter, 'He is going before you to Galilee; there you will see him, as he told you.'"

The gospel of the Lord.

All: **Praise to you Lord, Jesus Christ.**

Leader: Let us take time to share with one another how we "rejoice in the Lord." Please finish this sentence: "I rejoice in the Lord by. . . ." (Allow time for the participants to share with a partner or with the entire group.)

Conclude with a rousing song; for example, "I Want to Praise Your Name" by Bob Hurd, OCP Publications.

SAMPLE   BULLETIN   ANNOUNCEMENT

Enjoy a night of rousing family entertainment as you continue to help the Holy Name Youth Group raise money to support its outreach and ministry with

STRIKE UP THE BAND

What: A cavalcade of musical talent as the jazz bands, swing choirs, dance and drill teams, and orchestras from North High School and St. Joseph High School join forces for a special performance.

Who: Everyone is invited to enjoy the musical talents of our local teens.

When: Sunday, May 27 at 1:30 p.m.

Where: Holy Name Church

Why: The Holy Name Youth Group is raising money to support our local food pantry and homeless shelter.

How: Tickets are available at the youth ministry office or at the door. A maximum of 300 tickets will be sold, so get yours early!

Cost: $3 in advance
$5 on day of performance
All profits will be donated to charity.

STRIKE UP THE BAND EVALUATION

Name _____

1. How did you participate in the "Strike Up the Band" fundraiser?

2. Analyze the best and worst parts of the fundraiser.

3. How can this fundraiser be improved in the future?

4. What were some secondary benefits of this fundraiser?

Appendix

More Great Ideas for Fundraising

These ideas were submitted by youth ministers from across the nation.

Kiss the Cow

A youth group was trying to raise money to buy a cow for a poor family in Nicaragua. To do so, they found cutout bodies of a cow and pasted photos of the faces of several church leaders (pastor, associate pastor, principal, youth minister, coach) to replace the cow's head. They glued these new depictions on separate glass jars and lined them up on a table outside of Sunday Mass with the promise that whoever's jar was stuffed with the most money would be taken to a local farm and have to "kiss the cow" (right on the lips!). At this church, the pastor won in a landslide and followed through on the promise. This fundraiser was able to raise enough money to purchase three cows.

Birthday Party Hosts

Parents of children from ages four to ten often come to dread hosting birthday parties. What can they do to keep a group of kids busy for two hours, sometimes confined to the indoors or a small yard? A youth group in upstate New York became birthday party hosts, charging parents a fee to plan activities and chaperone parties for young children. Depending on the services asked for, this group often made between $50 and $100 for each party.

Bail Me Out

One group of teens redesigned their youth room as a "jail" and voluntarily imprisoned some fellow teens. It was the jailed teens' task to get bailed out by each raising $100. They did this by calling on the phone to family members, parishioners, and friends who were asked to make a pledge to "bail out" these jailed teens. This project also works well when teens capture and "imprison" prominent adults in your parish who are similarly asked to arrange bail.

Big Mac Booth

This kind of "Big Mac" involves a group of teenagers "capturing" an adult or other teen, bringing them to a place where a large mattress has been laid on the ground, and then "dog piling" on the person with the full force of, say, ten or twelve teenagers. This activity works well at a church bazaar or carnival. Just remind the teens that the Big Mac is all for show and they aren't really out to hurt their customers! The teens can sponsor the Big Mac Booth and sell "contracts" to capture and pile on top of unsuspecting people who are in attendance. One group charged $2 for each regular contract, but $5 for pulling off a "Big Mac" on the pastor, youth minister, coach, or mayor.

Raffle

Many parishioners, together with their businesses, are able to donate raffle prizes. One local pizza parlor offered the prize of one large pizza per week for one year. Another offered a year's supply of laundry and cleaning service. Teens can solicit donations of this kind and then make up and sell raffle tickets. The youth group is able to keep all of the profits.

Penny Carnival

Young children love a good carnival and are even more enamored when the carnival is created especially for them. Teens can turn their youth room into a simple penny carnival with games like a ring toss, fishing for a prize (children hold "fishing pole" with a clothespin attached over a barrier to win a small trinket), "tip the bottles" (with bean bags), and more. The games should be easily played by children under five. Award stickers or other small trinkets as prizes, and the kids will be as happy as can be. If possible, the teens can take this penny carnival on the road, setting up the games at a preschool or in a kindergarten classroom after arranging this with the teacher or administrator.

Breakfast With Santa

Teens dress up as elves while an appropriate adult Santa is chosen to host a breakfast for young children and their parents. A Christmas concert featuring a high school choir can accompany the event. Other teens prepare the meal—typically a selection of pastries and fruits. A typical admission for this event is $15 for parent and child.

Computer Tutorial

Teens are still way ahead of the older generations when it comes to being computer savvy. A church youth group in California recently hired themselves out as "computer tutors" helping adult parishioners set up home computers, learn basic word processing, navigate the world wide web, and other needed skills. Teens can charge by the hour or by the visit.

Yard Sales/Rummage Sales

This traditional fundraiser is different because it is completely organized by teenagers. They collect used household items, store them, and then arrange a day to sell what they have collected either outside of their youth room or inside the church auditorium.

Play and Pay Olympics

This is an outdoor event run by teens for teens. The "customers" pay to compete in each event. A record sheet is kept at each event for top scores. At the end of the "Olympics," winners of each event are awarded a prize. Some sample events: running an obstacle course for time, throwing a softball through a hula hoop thirty yards away, playing "home run derby" with a plastic ball and bat, and trying to kick a field goal through a goal post using a rubber dodge ball.

Ball-a-thon

Arrange for teens to get pledges for making basketball foul shots, 3-point shots, and half-court shots. For example, 25 cents for each free throw made, $1 for each three pointer, and $5 for the half-court variety.

Door Decorations

Have the teens contact local businesses to sponsor the doorway of the youth room, classrooms, or other doors on the school or parish grounds. For a predetermined donation, the business gets to advertise with its logo for a specific period of time.